*L*EARNING
Your Way Through
*C*OLLEGE

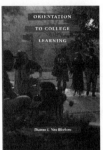

Also available from the Wadsworth College Success™ Series:

Orientation to College Learning (1995)
by Dianna L. Van Blerkom

I Know What It Says . . . What Does It Mean?
Critical Skills for Critical Reading (1995)
by Daniel J. Kurland

The Adult Learner's Guide to College Success,
Revised Edition (1995)
by Laurence N. Smith and Timothy L. Walter

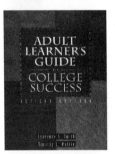

Your Transfer Planner: Strategic Tools and
Guerrilla Tactics (1995)
by Carey E. Harbin

Toolkit for College Success (1994)
by Daniel R. Walther

Pocket Toolkit (interactive software, 1994)
by Daniel R. Walther and Glaser Media Group

Mastering Mathematics: How to Be a Great
Math Student, Second Edition (1994)
by Richard Manning Smith

Turning Point (1993)
by Joyce D. Weinsheimer

Merlin: The Sorcerer's Guide to Survival in College (1990)
by Christopher F. Monte

Also available from the Freshman Year Experience℠ Series:

The Power to Learn: Helping Yourself to College Success
(1993)
by William E. Campbell

*To get your copies of the above Wadsworth titles,
please visit your local bookseller.*

LEARNING
Your Way Through
COLLEGE

Robert N. Leamnson
University of Massachusetts, Dartmouth

WADSWORTH PUBLISHING COMPANY

I(T)P™   AN INTERNATIONAL THOMSON PUBLISHING COMPANY

Belmont • Albany • Bonn • Boston • Cincinnati • Detroit • London
Madrid • Melbourne • Mexico City • New York • Paris • San Francisco
Singapore • Tokyo • Toronto • Washington

College Success Editor: *Angela Gantner Wrahtz*
Editorial Asistant: *Kate Peltier*
Production Editor: *Michelle Filippini*
Managing Designer: *Ann Butler*
Print Buyer: *Diana Spence*
Permissions Editor: *Robert Kauser*
Signing Representative: *Lisa Gebo*
Copy Editor: *Judith Abrams*
Cover and Text Design: *Christy Butterfield Design*
Compositor: *Christi Payne Fryday, Book Arts*
Printer: *Malloy Lithographing, Inc.*

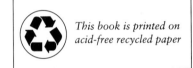

This book is printed on acid-free recycled paper

For more information, contact Wadsworth Publishing Company.

Wadsworth Publishing Company
10 Davis Drive
Belmont, California 94002, USA

International Thomson Publishing Europe
Berkshire House 168–173
High Holborn
London, WC1V 7AA, England

Thomas Nelson Australia
102 Dodds Street
South Melbourne 3205
Victoria, Australia

Nelson Canada
1120 Birchmount Road
Scarborough, Ontario
Canada M1K 5G4

International Thomson Editores
Campos Eliseos 385, Piso 7
Col. Polanco
11560 México D.F. México

International Thomson Publishing GmbH
Königswinterer Strasse 418
53227 Bonn, Germany

International Thomson Publishing Asia
221 Henderson Road
#05-10 Henderson Building
Singapore 0315

International Thomson Publishing Japan
Hirakawacho Kyowa Building, 3F
2-2-1 Hirakawacho
Chiyoda-ku, Tokyo 102, Japan

Library of Congress Cataloging-in-Publication Data
Leamnson, Robert N.
     Learning your way through college / Robert N. Leamnson
         p.   cm.
     Includes index.
     ISBN 0-534-24504-8 (alk. paper)
     1. College student orientation—Handbooks, manuals, etc. 2. Study skills—Handbooks, manuals, etc. I. Title.
LB2343.3.L43   1995
378.1'7'02812—dc20   94-24778

TO

my teachers

AND

my students

Contents

Eight   *Strategies*   83

Nine   *Exams*   97

Ten   *Autonomy*   111

Preface

his book was developing during a period when the need for better learning had once again captured public attention. There was, however, something new in the air this time: a stirring that continues to this day and offers hope for the long-range future. That new element is the growing interest, at the college level, in the art and science of teaching. Because we are just now in the midst of this change, no one can tell what the many current programs to improve college teaching will produce. What is clear is that college students will soon be noticing the effects, whatever they are. Should it come to pass that a significant number of college teachers adopt a conversational, discursive, or recitative style, and begin using writing for its learning as well as its evaluative aspects, and present their disciplines in a problem-solving or case-study manner, students may well find the transition from high school to college more shocking than it is now.

That the high school/college transition might become worse is cause for worry. For well over a decade, John Gardner and others have spent themselves in heroic efforts to ferry students over this cultural gap. What has actually happened on college campuses in consequence of their efforts is something of a mixed bag. To offer some rationale for yet another book on learning, it will be necessary to look at two types of transition programs that represent, admittedly, the extremes of the spectrum.

A number of colleges have initiated skills programs for first-year students, sometimes optional and sometimes required for students considered to be at risk. Typically the skills emphasized are study, reading, writing, time management, critical thinking, note taking, test taking, goal setting, and dealing with stress. A characteristic element in these courses, which puts them at one end of the spectrum, is that they do not have traditional academic content of the kind that would ordinarily reside in a department of a college. The syllabus for this type of course will make no mention of historical events, works of poetry, or the principles of economics, biology, philosophy, or music. There is a logic in the development of these courses that is based on the analysis of an educated person—one well versed in the ways of learning. An analysis of educated people would show them to have just those skills listed in the syllabus of a skills course. Skills courses appear to be based on the premise that the skillful learner can be synthesized by the independent and content-free development of those skills discovered during the analysis. The student is being prepared to be a learner. Skills courses are being conducted in many colleges and might be thought of as experiments in progress.

At the other end of the spectrum are the first-year seminars or colloquia. These take a very different approach and seem to be, consciously or otherwise, following the lead of Mortimer Adler, who suggested that anyone can learn serious material if it comes at a reasonable pace and if the learner gets a lot of coaching and practice. The first-year seminar that I have in mind always has some academic content, but it is not a survey course. In fact, the typical content is highly delineated, resembling at first glance that of a senior-level course. The content might be the writings of a single author, the various ways different authors have treated one brief period of history, or any other well-defined topic. The range of topics that can be taught in first-year seminars is enormous, and that makes them attractive to regular academic faculty who happen to have something they would dearly like to talk about in detail. To serve their purpose as transition courses, however, first-year seminars require pedagogy that will indeed develop the required skills as the content matter is pursued. How to ensure this pedagogy is far from certain, but faculty development will no doubt figure largely if this approach is to succeed. Freshman seminars are, therefore, experiments in progress as well, but the current interest that college presidents and provosts are showing in improving undergraduate teaching by all faculty is reassuring.

I have tried to produce a book that will prove useful to students no matter what kind of orientation course or seminar they encounter, and equally useful to other students who do not have the benefit of any such orientation course. It is, in other words, not a textbook. My intent was to produce something like a handbook that can be used in conjunction with any content or skills course a student might take. It is, therefore, neither a treatise on learning nor an exercise book for practicing skills. The "audience in my head" was the average student about to take college courses in traditional disciplines, or the student already taking these courses and wondering why things aren't going well. The chapter titles were kept simple and topical in order to direct students immediately to the most common sources of academic problems: what they are actually doing during class, what they do between classes, how they do assignments, how they interact with their teachers, how they prepare for and take exams, and their attitude toward learning in general. This makes demands on the student, because the advice must be quite general if it is to be applicable to all disciplines. It is left to the student, for example, to apply any useful ideas on keeping notes to whatever courses he is taking and to the idiosyncrasies of his various teachers. This approach is consistent with a general theme of the book, which is that serious learning is not particularly easy and will require a certain ingenuity in responding to the demands of the moment.

I set out to write a book of ideas and advice. Because it is for students, I felt no need to justify the recommended approaches by referring specifically to authoritative sources. It should not be inferred from this fact that all the notions and ideas expressed derive entirely from the opinions of the author. In fact, it is unlikely that there is an original idea anywhere in the book. There is, on the other hand, such an enormous array of authorities on learning, not always in agreement with one another, that one must still, in the end, make choices. I have not referenced my sources in this book because I did not believe doing so would help students, who are its intended primary audience. Some readers will nonetheless see the influence of Jacques Barzun, Mortimer Adler, Neil Postman, and Arnold Arons throughout the general-learning portions of the text. The ideas on language have their origins in the writing of Walter J. Ong and Lev Vygostsky, refreshed and revitalized by the redoubtable Neil Postman. The recent literature on writing is immense, but I owe much to the work of Stephen Tchudi, James Britton, and Sondra Perl. Many ideas in Chapter 8, "Strategies," came from Richard Light's research, and permeating the whole is a general theory of cognitive science derived from the work of John Searle, Christopher Wills, Jean-Pierre Changeux, E. O. Wilson, Owen Flannagan, and Gerald Edelman. The work of these scholars is generally read by their colleagues, or by college faculty and graduate students. Undergraduates normally benefit only in an indirect way: when their own teachers happen to incorporate these ideas into their teaching. I find this latter fact unfortunate.

My intent, therefore, was to put the scholarly work directly into the hands of students, not in the form of research as such, but reformulated as advice. A lot of things can go wrong here. Students accustomed to modern textbooks seem unsure as to what to do with a book consisting only of words. It has even made a few teachers uneasy. Such a book also assumes a reader with a certain level of comprehension to begin with. Learning to learn is a classic chicken-egg problem, and in the case of a book on learning to learn, much hangs on the language level at which it is cast. Having in mind a first- or second-year college student of any age but with average preparation, I tried to prepare a text that would be comprehensible to the intended readers, but only with some effort on their part. If those kind student reviewers who found the level appropriate are representative of the target audience, perhaps the book will find a niche.

I am grateful to Brian and Ann Wilkie, Raymond Dumont, and Catherine Houser for their encouragement and their expert advice on early drafts; to my editors at Wadsworth, Angie Gantner Wrahtz, Kate Peltier, and Michelle Filippini; and to the many reviewers who made valuable suggestions. Sincere thanks, finally, to Lisa Gebo, who first prodded me into preparing the material for publication.

Robert N. Leamnson
North Dartmouth, Massachusetts
April 1994

LEARNING
Your Way Through
COLLEGE

one

College

Student Voices

IN HIGH SCHOOL I NEVER CRACKED A BOOK. I HAD A
B AVERAGE. I'VE BEEN HERE THREE MONTHS AND I'VE
DROPPED ONE CLASS AND I'M FAILING TWO OTHERS.
THERE'S SOMETHING WRONG WITH THIS PLACE.

—TIM

adio, TV, magazines, and newspapers have conditioned us to expect that every question has an answer, and one that is short and simple. New college students will have questions about the new place they are entering, and are likely to want short and simple answers. College, however, is a place of long explanations. To preview this world of long answers, I have chosen four sample questions from the many that students might ask, and will use these to demonstrate the kind of reflective investigation you will find typical of college work.

1. What's this place like?
2. What can college do for me?
3. What will I have to do here?
4. How is this different from what went before?

These questions can be approached in a superficial way, or they can be used to probe deeply into the college experience.

What's This Place Like?

The first question is really a bundle of questions. The dorm student is probably asking, "Can I choose my own roommate? What's the food like? Are there games on the mainframe? Do they have concerts on campus?" The commuter will be asking, "What's the bus service like? Where can I get lunch? Is there a place to hang out between classes?" Academically, all will want to know about library use, availability of computers, their course schedules, what the faculty is like, where to find tutors, and what the "killer" courses are.

Except for the one about faculty, these questions have short, uncomplicated answers. But short and simple answers don't really tell you enough about this unique place called college. To illustrate the kind of answers you will come to expect in college, I will invent a hypothetical entity, called your Personal Guru. Your Guru is actually a composite of the many wise people you will encounter during your college years. Some will be faculty or family; others can be found in the library or the administration, or among the staff and the other students. If your instincts are good, you will recognize a wise person when you encounter one.

For now, suppose we ask this hypothetical Personal Guru our first question, "What's this place like?" Because your Guru is hypothetical and because no one has been able to distill all university wisdom into one place, we don't know exactly how the Guru would answer, but we can probably predict the general form the answers would take. Personal Guru would likely rub her chin or stroke his beard and say something like "Well, what we have here is an adult community of scholars." Not what you expected; welcome to the world of long explanations.

You're being told that you are entering other people's world. It is a world of reading, study, talking, writing, and spreading the word when true and interesting things are learned or discovered. Much of what we associate with college—the social life, athletics, school newspapers, and the dozens of clubs and organizations—has sprung up to support the central activity: students learning from books, from the faculty, from support personnel, and from one another.

The subtle message here is one that many students discover on their own and puzzle over. High school seemed to exist for—to have been designed around—the student. College, on the other hand, sometimes seems to have an independent existence. It moves along on its own and is quite willing to let newcomers jump aboard, but only if they want to. Your Guru is introducing you to an idea that will come up time and again: College is there to be used. The intent is not so much to process students as to provide them the opportunity to join a learning community.

This aspect of college helps explain another of its characteristics: Different students react to college in widely different ways. One takes to it like the proverbial duckling to water; it's exhilarating from the start and just gets better. Another finds it a foreign and unfriendly place, and leaves after a year or so. It's the same college in both cases; the difference must be in the students. The difference is very often neither in intelligence nor in preparation. Having an appropriate attitude toward this new place and being willing to adjust to it are the more important factors. What the Guru is telling you is that what this place is like is less important than how you react to it.

What Can College Do for Me?

Most students come to college with fairly firm ideas as to what college should do for them. It should expand their circle of friends, provide them with a degree, and prepare them for a high-paying job. Your Guru might respond, "College will unsettle your mind and change your life." Many new students are not sure they like the sound of that! "Is it a good idea to unsettle my mind? Do I want my life changed?" Again, this line is just the opening line of a long explanation of what college actually can do for you.

Most of us start college thinking of it as a place to get answers. Answers should settle the mind, not unsettle it. But college really is a place of long explanations, and part of the explanation, very often, is that many questions don't have simple answers. Questions are often situational, and even the simple-sounding ones are frequently entangled in a prickly context. Poke a simple question and you're likely to send ripples through a huge net of interconnections with things you hadn't thought of. Most interesting questions don't have simple answers, and college is concerned mostly with interesting questions.

Unsettling the mind means becoming discontent with simplistic answers. The unsettled mind is an active mind, always searching.

Similarly, changing your life is mostly a matter of readjusting your attitudes as a result of learning. College is a period or four or five years you set aside for your personal development. A lot can be done in four years. You can learn a new sport or a new language, change your appearance, or even change your tastes—but these things could just as easily be done outside college. This book will focus on what only college can do for you during these four years.

The best thing college can do for you is to prepare you for a lifetime of learning. Again, this may not sit well with some new students. To anyone who considers learning a tiresome and annoying chore, to be done as quickly and effortlessly as possible, a lifetime of it doesn't sound all that appealing. But one thing college can do is change your mind about learning itself. What if it isn't really a chore? What if learning new things turns out to be enjoyable?

We do change our minds, whether we like to admit it or not. We drift away from people who at one time were our best friends; we change our hairstyles, the way we dress, and the way we speak. College is the right place to open your mind to the possibility of changing your attitudes about any number of things, including learning. But changing your mind is itself a process of learning, which brings us to the next question.

What Will I Have to Do Here?

When I started college, my own Personal Guru told me, "Learn everything you can." It seemed bland advice from a guru. As usual, there was a long answer; it involved discovering that learning meant something quite different to my teachers than it did to me.

In college you need to do a lot more than just be there. The prime task of the college student—the essential thing you must do—is to learn to learn. *Learning to learn* is a strange expression. It seems to describe a closed circle—if you're not already into it, how do you get started? One is tempted to make it seem easier by using such expressions as *discovering the secret of learning*. But this is misleading. There isn't any secret of learning—no trick that some conspiracy has been hiding from students. Nor is *discovering* an appropriate word, suggesting as it does that you can stumble onto the way to learn by chance and without effort. Learning to learn is a chicken-egg problem, but not an insoluble one. This book was written to help you jump into the "learning circle." The goal is to become a *learning person*. Once you become a learning person, learning things becomes a joy.

Even so, learning to learn is included here under things *you* have to do. College provides you with the appropriate environment, with all the tools you need, and with instructions as to how to proceed. Neither college nor any other outside agent, however, can *cause* you to learn. You yourself are the "cause" of learning.

These are not exactly comforting words. College begins to look like a "do-it-yourself" project. That's largely true, but if you've ever finished a "do-it-yourself" project, you know the satisfaction it can bring. Whether it's rebuilding a carburetor or patching your own jeans, you appreciate it more, enjoy it more, and understand it better than if you'd simply paid someone else to do it.

You also come to appreciate help and advice. Doing it yourself doesn't mean doing it all alone. Moms, dads, big brothers or sisters, and friends can all lend a hand. It may be just a matter of showing interest or providing advice, or it may mean actually taking part in the project. In any event, help is always appreciated and makes the job even more satisfying. Much the same can be said of college learning.

How Is This Different from What Went Before?

How does college differ from high school? This is certainly one of the most serious questions a new student can ask, and one that requires a long answer. Since only about half the students who start college will stay and be graduated, it's clear that college is not just four more years of what went before. Getting readjusted for college work is such a challenge for so many students that there's a common term for it: *the transition problem.*

How difficult the transition is will depend to some extent on what you were doing just before college. Most new students enter college directly from high school, but more and more people are entering after having worked for some years or perhaps having raised a family. Both groups face a transition, but it is usually less abrupt for the older students. In general, students coming to college directly from high school face a more difficult adjustment.

One might expect the opposite—the longer the time away from school, the more difficult the transition. That expectation is based on the assumption that the major difficulty in college is the content of the coursework, and that recent experience in a classroom is the best preparation. That assumption is suspect on both counts. The most likely candidate for failure in college is not the student who has been away from the classroom for a while, but one who never experiences a *need to know.* Time away from school does not necessarily reduce the need and desire to learn; it's just as likely to increase them. Nor does time spent in a classroom necessarily increase the desire to learn. Depending on what goes on there, it may well stifle curiosity and deaden interest. Nontraditional students are also more likely to come to college expecting something quite different from their recent life, and so be prepared to make adjustments. Recent high school graduates can be lulled into believing that college is just four more years of the same.

With a few notable exceptions, colleges are quite different from high school. The obvious differences—more buildings, a department for each subject, classes only three days a week, and so on—are not the important ones. What is important is that high school and college have defined their functions differently. High schools are largely organized to provide an experience, whereas colleges provide only an opportunity. This is a serious difference for the students. When an experience is provided, you need only submit to it, or perhaps sit back and enjoy it. An opportunity, on the other hand, is simply there—waiting for you to do something. A heavy diet of externally provided experiences induces passivity. Opportunities are lost on the passive. What this means in practical terms is that a lot of new students enter college expecting to "get an education," but in the high school sense of having something done to them by someone else. College teachers, on the other hand, see education as something students do to themselves. Such a situation can easily lead to mutual misunderstanding. The change from passive recipient of an experience to active pursuer of opportunity is the most difficult transition for the new student.

This change from *being provided for* to *providing for oneself* permeates all aspects of college life. From getting to class on time and taking care of the laundry to completing a senior thesis, college students must learn to cope without continual supervision. Most colleges allow students a great deal of freedom, and to most recent high school graduates, freedom sounds good.

Again, the older returning students may have an advantage here, because they have more likely already learned that freedom is a two-edged sword. Increased freedom implies more choices, but choices have consequences. No matter what you may have heard, making choices is dead easy. What's difficult is anticipating the consequences of choices and accepting responsibility afterward. Almost everything we do is a matter of choice. We can choose to shower or stay dirty, to get up or stay in bed, to hang out or write a lab report. Each of those choices, however, has a consequence. The more choices you have, the more complicated life becomes, because you have more consequences to anticipate and more responsibilities to bear. Learning to live with a lot of new choices is a huge factor in the college transition.

When education is presented as an opportunity and not as an experience, making responsible choices is the only option. Opportunities must be chosen. Whoever first said that opportunity knocks overstated the case in my opinion. It's certainly not true that all you need to do is open the door! What opportunity really does is lie there waiting for some quick-witted, ambitious soul to come along.

The wonderful thing about college as opportunity is that it's never used up. No matter how many students take advantage of it, the opportunity is still available to the rest. Again, however, the expression *taking advantage* needs thinking about. Is it easy? Do you just grab the thing and run?

In fact, taking advantage of the actual opportunity that college provides is not easy. In nearly every chapter of this book you'll encounter some variation on the same theme: Education is a matter of self-induced change—something you do to yourself—that is at the same time both satisfying and difficult. A major hurdle for the new student is the transition from passive recipient of an educational experience to active self-educator.

The Rewards

Few things gladden the heart of a college teacher more than the student who catches fire, so to speak, and breaks into the learning-to-learn cycle. Anyone who has stayed in school long enough to become a teacher must have rediscovered the child's curiosity about how things work and how things got to be the way they are. It's quite wonderful to see that curiosity reawakened in a college student. When a student begins lurking about a faculty member's office, looking for books and asking a lot of questions, you can be sure that he has reawakened that long-dormant curiosity and is rediscovering the joy of indulging it.

Teacher satisfaction is not the central point here, of course. I mention it because the true goal of the best teachers is to make themselves dispensable. Teachers do not make themselves dispensable by "teaching" their students everything they'll ever need to know. They do it by getting young people to the point where they can learn without teachers. Such people are enabled; their future is something they will determine, not simply endure. If, during your college years, you become so enabled—so liberated—you will have done what you came here to do. You will have remade yourself.

two

Learning

Student Voices

THIS COURSE HAS *NOTHING* TO DO WITH MY MAJOR.
NO ONE TAKES THESE DISTRIBUTION REQUIREMENTS
SERIOUSLY. WHY IS SHE BEING SUCH A HARD-NOSE?

—VINNY

 ollege is an invitation to grow, but it is only an invitation. Entering students are presented with choices; they will not march in lockstep through a common set of guaranteed learning experiences. The college experience will vary from student to student because there are differences between majors, between courses, and between teachers. Freedom includes the option to choose one course rather than another, or this teacher and not that one. Freedom, then, can have a dark side. The freedom to choose includes the freedom to choose poorly. You are free to not grow during your college years, to choose not to be challenged—to leave college degreed but not educated.

Emerging from college uneducated is a grim prospect. It is possible, however, because unwise choices can have long-term consequences. You are free to start your day at ten o'clock, but the consequence might be that you miss the most useful courses and the best teachers. You can even choose the way you go about learning, and that choice will certainly have far-reaching consequences.

Approaches to Learning

There are indeed different ways to learn. Some learning is quite mechanical. Learning in this mechanical sense is committing things to memory and is much like entering text or data into a computer. To learn this way is to store for retrieval. You "enter" the six parts of this, or the four causes of that, or the dates for so-and-so, "recall" several times to see that nothing has been lost, and "exit." "Learning" has been done. Brain circuitry, however, unlike that of computers, appears to be in a state of continual flux. You may have stored material for a history course, but moving to a chemistry assignment, watching TV, or having lunch tends to muddle that carefully stored historical data. Considered as a computer, the brain is disturbingly imperfect. And considered as a brain, a computer is grossly inadequate. Only in fiction do computers understand what they store. Computers do not associate meaning with the symbols they manipulate with such breathtaking speed and unerring accuracy. Lacking understanding, computers cannot respond to questions that begin with *How* or *Why*. They cannot be said to learn in the flexible and reflective way that humans must. Treating your brain as if it were a computer wastes its enormous potential.

Imagine your surprise if a teacher announced that laptop computers would be allowed during exams. You would likely prepare by feeding as much information as you could into the computer. Some college teachers go even further—they allow books and notes to be used during exams. New students usually welcome that news with sighs of relief—at least they do the first time. Seniors in physics or philosophy usually groan, knowing that they are in for a grueling test of comprehension and understanding. College students soon come to know that teachers who give open-book exams are not excusing them from learning. They are only sparing the brain the tiresome and inefficient toil of storing great quantities of information. What all those facts and data mean and how they can be used in new and challenging situations still need to be learned.

None of which should be taken to mean that the ability to store and retrieve information is not useful or, in some cases, necessary. It's not possible, for example, to have a sensible conversation without facts to draw on. Nor is the brain used up or worn out by storing a small encyclopedia of baseball statistics or an epic poem. Furthermore, some of your teachers may indeed place great value on your talent for storing and retrieving information. It is one way of learning. It can be a comfortable trap, however, if you substitute it for the more serious kind of learning that the best college teachers expect. That some teachers give open-book tests surely demonstrates that they expect the student to do more than store and retrieve information.

Recognition

There is a second way of learning that may have served you well for many years but will prove insufficient in college. It consists of refining to a high degree our natural talent for recognizing. Recognizing a face, a name, or a word can be seductively comforting. Recognition implies familiarity. The unfamiliar causes an uneasy tension; the familiar makes us comfortable. In fact, the great relief we feel when moving from the totally unknown to terrain we recognize as familiar may be too comforting for our own good. We tend to be satisfied with recognizing, and see no need for anything more.

To merely recognize something as familiar is in fact the absolute minimum that would qualify as knowledge. It's the smallest step above complete ignorance. Still, small step that it is, it is sufficiently rewarding that we are seduced into the comforting belief that we do indeed know something new. We become complacent. To be familiar with the French Revolution, for example, might mean knowing that it took place in the late eighteenth century and little more. Maybe this is what is meant by the adage "A little knowledge is a dangerous thing."

Minimal though it is, recognition knowledge, in addition to providing internal comfort, often brings external rewards as well. A game-show contestant can win a roomful of furniture by recognizing that the Albert who discovered relativity was Einstein and not Schweitzer. A student receives a valued, if less gaudy, reward for the same kind of recognition on a multiple-choice test. This weak kind of learning has come to be generously rewarded, and therefore highly valued, because it is very easily tested.

Contrary to a common student belief, teachers do not enjoy giving exams. Writing questions is tiresome; reading and grading answers, a dreaded chore. That is why the multiple-choice exam, probably a necessity when large numbers of students are being tested, has become commonplace even where it is not easily justified. In some classes it is the only kind of examination ever encountered. While it is possible to design a challenging multiple-choice exam which would demand thorough understanding on the part of the student, in practice most of them test only recognition. The phenomenal popularity of the multiple-choice test will have profound significance for new college students should they encounter, as is likely, a sizable number of college teachers who are not content with recognition learning. These teachers are looking for understanding and for students who "know how to think." They expect facts and data to be used to support a position or argument. To merely recall or recognize the facts will not satisfy these teachers. Success in college will almost certainly demand that you raise your sights well above recognition learning. Far too many teachers will expect more than the vague familiarity that characterizes recognition knowledge.

Even if it somehow turned out that all of your teachers were satisfied with recall and recognition, you would be missing an enormous opportunity if information storage and retrieval were the only demands you made on yourself during your college year. Stored knowledge simply does not provide adequately for the demands of living. A surprising number of working people will tell you that in their work they never use any specific information that they acquired in college. Their college experience was important not for the information, which in many disciplines becomes obsolete, but for the habits of mind that enable them to cope with a multitude of original problems that spring up without warning. What is this wonderful faculty—this capacity for figuring things out, for distinguishing between fact and folklore, between what's useful and what's irrelevant? How do we develop it?

Beyond Storing, Retrieving, and Recognizing

The truly educated have been relieved of the difficult burden of having to believe everything they are told. To anyone who has always believed that great virtue lay in a talent for remembering everything they were told, that statement will likely sound cynical or even subversive. But though it is not often stated quite so boldly, the idea it expresses is widely held; it is certainly not original. Robert Benchley suggested the same thing many years ago when he stated that the purpose of being educated was to "know when a man is talking rot." There is nothing subversive or cynical here. Simply put, the message is that an educated person will be able to decipher the exact meaning of the spoken or written word; facts will not lie dormant in her head, but will spring forward to guide a logical analysis of what is heard or read.

Consider the example of the employer who quieted a complaining group of employees by reminding them that although they had just received a 10 percent raise, his salary had risen only 5 percent. For those who had always found percentages too tiring to think about, there was no answer to this seemingly flawless logic. Only the educated person could ask, "Five percent *of what,* sir?" A rare case, perhaps, but to be unable to figure things out, or to recognize nonsense for what it is, is to be condemned to a kind of mental slavery—to being a potential victim for clever manipulators.

Many of your college teachers, no matter what their area of special interest, will want for you an education that *enables*: one that empowers you to mobilize facts and use them to build arguments, proofs, and refutations. Such an education is the product of a higher-order learning—something beyond recall and recognition.

New Expectations

Those of your teachers who value serious learning will be happy to be your guides on the path toward this higher-order learning. The college provides teachers who are themselves well educated: they have spent considerable time learning a great deal about an area of special interest. Some of these teachers, however, are a source of great confusion for new students. Paradoxically, it is often the brightest, the most knowledgeable, and the most scholarly teachers who cause the greatest distress. When a new student is baffled by a college teacher, it is almost certainly because the teacher and the student are at cross-purposes. The student's efforts are not matching the teacher's expectations.

New college students, no matter what their age, tend to see their teachers as repositories of information. Teachers, however, see themselves as guides leading students out of uncertainty and into the world of the mind. Perhaps no one should be surprised if, when the two meet in the classroom, there is often mutual misunderstanding. Students who have total recall of the facts find their efforts unappreciated. These teachers seem always to expect something more. If you and your classmates find yourselves saying, "I don't know what she wants!" you have most likely had the good fortune to meet one of the many teachers who are looking for something more.

What this "something more" is cannot be briefly described, as were the more elementary ways of learning. It is a high-level way of learning that will become clearer as you proceed through these pages, and as you become familiar with your teachers and come to understand the reading, writing, and problem solving they ask of you, and the kinds of performance they reward on exams. Certainly one element will wind its way through every aspect of the deeper and more reflective learning we have described; that element is language.

The World of Words and the World of Things

Seeing the Connection

More than a few college teachers have reminded their classes, now and then with a touch of exasperation, "The words mean something!" This plea is an attempt to impress on students that words represent real things, real actions, and real events—that they are not mere symbols that can be sorted and arranged arbitrarily. The full meaning of the message is often missed because everyone already knows that words carry meaning and we show evidence of it constantly. If we are told that we will be paid on Friday, we will certainly show up when the real Friday rolls around, expecting to be paid in real money.

Nevertheless, teachers are puzzled because that same tight linkage between words and real things does not always hold in the classroom. When a student of physics does a calculation to determine the weight of a large fishing boat and reports that the weight is two ten-thousandths of an ounce, it is clear that the relation between physics and real boats has been lost.

This example illustrates a major obstacle to serious learning. For whatever reasons, many students have come to believe that words used in school do not have the same connection to reality that they have in everyday life. In a cartoon that hangs on many a professor's door, a teacher proclaims that Hitler was one of the truly great humanitarians of all time and watches in dismay as the students dutifully record this "fact" in their notes. A failure to question the preposterous statement demonstrates that for the listener, the words no longer relate to anything real. It is essential for you to learn quickly that "school language" describes reality as surely as does your day-to-day conversation. To have Generals Grant and Lee fighting in the American Revolution is not merely a problem of arranging the words improperly. The statement proclaims a belief and demonstrates a profound confusion about real people doing real things in real time.

Students and teachers arrive at a meeting of the minds when students get beyond recording and manipulating words as symbols and come to envision the reality the words represent. Like a great many other things, dealing with the meanings behind words instead of the words themselves is a matter of practice. Much of your college education will be a matter of practice with the language.

Finding the Right Words

Students who come to associate words with real things or concepts may still find themselves struggling with a second language problem. They find that what went into the head smoothly does not come out quite so easily. "I know it, but I can't say it." Again, it is often in the classrooms of the better teachers that this problem is most acute. A teacher who knows the subject uncommonly well and has a great command of the language can present quite complex ideas in a way that makes them go down like honey. After a disastrous exam, students are heard to say, "It was so simple when *she* did it."

Students who have this difficulty can be said to "know" in the sense that they recognize something as familiar. That familiar thing touches other familiar things and sends notions, glimpses, and pale images skittering through the head. At such a time a student can often remember exactly where the teacher stood when the elusive argument was presented. They can almost see the page in their notes. Still, the words will not come. The cause of this inability to nail down what we are sure we know is not all that mysterious. When we can't express familiar ideas, it's because, familiar though they are, they have never really been verbalized.

If you are truly to progress beyond recall or recognition learning, you must become adept at verbalizing ideas—it must become nearly automatic. Teachers have to be good at verbalizing ideas. Students, all too frequently, are content with merely remembering the words the teacher generated. But what if that isn't possible? What if you find yourself burdened, or blessed, with a number of teachers who transmit ideas in an avalanche of words, illustrations, and examples—far too many to get onto paper? If these teachers are also good storytellers, you might find yourself soaking up the concepts, the arguments, the big picture—but not paying much attention to the words. You might well say of such a teacher, "He really knows how to explain things," or "She makes it easy." But when the time comes for you to do the explaining, the words are not there. Where did that wonderful and clear explanation go?

If a teacher can hold your attention as we've just described, she certainly won't be reading from her notes or reciting them from memory. What she is doing is generating language—literally making it up—language that represents the ideas in her head. This is a skill that good teachers either have a knack for or develop early on. The question here is: Is she doing something that you can't? No. She is verbalizing, and you can do it with practice. In fact, if you find yourself, as in the example, concentrating on the ideas and arguments—the big picture instead of the words—then you have already made the first big step. You are concentrating on ideas and not merely words.

Verbalizing

Verbalizing is not just speaking or writing. A tape deck is not verbalizing when it plays back a message, nor is a computer verbalizing when it prints a page of text. A person reciting a speech from memory is certainly speaking, but would not be verbalizing in the sense intended here. Verbalizing is finding, linking, and expressing appropriate words in such a way that they accurately transmit an idea. If you have ever been called on, without warning, to give a speech, you know what verbalizing is and how difficult it can be. It's what teachers expect when they call on you for an explanation or an elaboration. The difficulty of verbalizing is evidenced when we respond to questions with one-word answers, or interrupt ourselves again and again with "You know?"

Getting a correct idea and putting together the language that will express it constitute the essence of learning. For the student who has gotten over the first language hurdle—seeing the meaning, the pictures, and the ideas behind the words—generating language to get those same ideas across to someone else is just the next step. Taking that step, however, requires two things: an appropriate vocabulary and a great deal of practice. There's no substitute for knowing the meaning of words: the more the better. Once you've acquired correct ideas and the vocabulary you need to express them, the rest is just a matter of practice.

Practice

Writing would seem like a good way to practice verbalizing, but I would recommend that you start with speaking. Writing is a private activity; there is no immediate feedback to let you know how you're doing. Talking to a teacher or another student provides an immediate response. Both thinking and language can be fine-tuned on the spot. A good way to start is to prepare, outside of class, some question that you would like answered or discussed. Ask your question in class when the opportunity arises. Asking a question in class requires great courage of a new student. But doing a brave thing can make a permanent change for the good. Exhilarating activities such as skydiving and downhill skiing had to start with a single brave act.

Asking a prepared question is somewhat contrived, but it will help you to get over that first-time terror. After a few warmup questions, you'll find that talking about the subject matter gets easier each time and can provide its own touch of exhilaration.

Integrative Learning

At their most demanding, your college teachers will expect you to extract ideas from their words, to put your understanding into language of your own, and one thing more: to relate knowledge from different disciplines. Reality is not organized in the way academic disciplines are. There are not separate worlds of economics, history, philosophy, and physics. All the rules and laws of all the areas of human inquiry are always and in all places at work in the same single world. For our purposes, this means that what you learn in chemistry remains true in biology, and biology cannot be ignored in sociology.

Fortunately, the doing of even this high level of learning is again a matter of practice. Should the topic of neural inhibition come up in psychology, that is the same physical phenomenon that was learned about in biology. Use what you already know to make sense of the new material. In this case, practice is mostly a matter of careful listening for familiar topics and words. If you hear that something has a certain probability of happening, that is the very same probability you learned about in math class. Probability does not become a different concept because it appears in anthropology. Integrative learning is mostly a matter of believing that what you have learned is universally true and can be used anywhere, any time.

Motivation

To say that conceptualizing from language, verbalizing ideas, and integrating knowledge are all a matter of practice is not to say that they are easy. You will soon learn that classroom learning is anything but restful. But how do you get yourself "up" for a subject? How do you motivate yourself to expend the necessary energy?

We tend to think that motivation is something we either have or don't have. This unfortunate belief encourages far too many new students to simply wait for the motivation to come along. What comes along, however, is usually fear—not the best motivating agent.

We fear failure or poor grades, and the embarrassment they bring. This may drive us to work harder. But fear is not compatible with the clear, rational thinking we need to learn well. It is also an emotion that is intense for short periods, but cannot—and clearly should not—be sustained. Fear kicks in a day or two before an exam is scheduled or a paper is due; it prompts frantic, but not always profitable, activity.

The best learning takes place when the mind is focused. When our mental powers are brought to bear on a problem in an effective way, the mind seems to act like a variable-beam flashlight—the kind that can illuminate a broad range of things dimly or can be focused to illuminate one thing very intensely. In our normal relaxed state, we are conscious of everything going on around us, but just barely so, as if it were all taking place in dim light. But when something truly engages our mind, our broad beam of superficial attention becomes focused on that single thing. Everything else is blocked out. It's difficult to distract someone who is truly focused on something of interest.

Such concentration is seldom motivated by fear. It comes from an intense need: not the need to avoid embarrassment, but the need to understand—to know this thing. The need to know is as powerful a force for learning as you are likely to encounter. The need to know should not be confused with the need for a diploma. Needing a degree will drive us to pay tuition, live away from home, eat dorm food, study for exams, and put up with a lot. But the diploma is a long-range goal, and easy to forget when you're struggling with European history or eighteenth-century poetry. You are indeed required to get passing grades in your courses to be awarded a diploma, but you can remember enough history or poetry to get a passing grade and still miss all the wonder and magic these topics can offer. When courses are merely to be endured and passed, the college experience becomes a long, boring bingo game. Semester after semester and year after year, the hapless student fills in line after line of the transcript, and at the end receives the prize. But once a student has felt the need to know and understand, learning becomes the goal and the diploma takes its proper place as documentation only. Satisfying a need to know is continually rewarding. Education becomes a matter of indulging our curiosity.

We have all experienced a need to know. One young man sought and located the woman he would eventually marry, knowing only her first name and the fact that she was enrolled at a college with some 40,000 students. That he followed many blind leads and spent many hours at his task goes without saying. Clearly this was a man driven by his need to know. Such a need seems to take control of the mind. We will do what it takes to satisfy that need.

Studying history is not quite the same as finding "lady love," however. Is it possible to discover, or at least generate, a similar kind of intense need to know when the subject is economics or biology? In truth, many times we have to create the need, and sometimes by artificial means. One way to stir up curiosity and a need to know is to become attuned to a teacher who is himself all fired up. You might wonder, for example, why an otherwise normal mature person goes all misty-eyed over the hydrogen bond. You can put that minimal amount of curiosity to good purpose. Find out what it is that has this guy so worked up!

Interest

It's tempting to explain away enthusiasm as a matter of interest. A curious word, *interest*. We all know when we have it and, just as unhesitatingly, when we don't. Seldom investigated is the question, "How did we get the interests we have and not others?" Interests are not something we're born with; they're not genetic traits. Interests, in fact, are learned. You can't be interested in something you know nothing about—and that makes for a fascinating puzzle. Students easily excuse themselves for not learning something because it is not interesting. But if interest is not possible until you've learned something about the subject, how do you ever get started? The chicken-egg problem arises in this instance because something thought to be true is not true at all. The assumption that some kind of "natural" interest is required in order to learn is simply not true. With a little discipline, you can learn enough about any topic to find out why others find it fascinating.

A more pleasant interpretation of the adage "A little knowledge is a dangerous thing" might be that a little knowledge can easily get you hooked. One young man took to reading the poetry of T. S. Eliot because his chemistry professor had been reading Eliot's poetry while proctoring an exam. Curiosity got the better of that young man. I doubt he ever regretted indulging that small curiosity. Don't dismiss any subject or topic as uninteresting until you know something about it.

When curiosity leads to a need to know, we approach books, assignments, lectures, and study in a new and dramatically different way. Reading loses the feel of duty and becomes a way to satisfy a need. The dutiful student reads paragraphs, pages, and chapters; the curious student explores topics, theories, ideas, and arguments.

The best way to stimulate a need to know is to listen or read with focused attention. Focusing your attention will pull the meaning from behind the words. Discovering meaning can provide just enough knowledge to kindle a little blaze. After that, interest will take care of itself.

Tickling the Brain

Students who enter college motivated by visions of the good life down the road find those distant dreams too remote in time to provide the day-to-day motivation for learning. Not many of us can find an immediate connection between electrical circuits in Physics 101 and that far-off comfortable house in the suburbs. It's best not to try. The secret, instead, is to wonder about how circuits work. Why does a circuit breaker trip? Does it know something? How does your thermostat know when to tell the furnace to switch on? Does it "feel" cold? Is wondering about things something special to science majors, or a mysterious gift of the very bright? I prefer to think that the very bright got that way by paying attention to their little curiosities and trying to get to the bottom of things.

I further suspect that people who are curious about a lot of things and poke about in books, indulging that curiosity, have simply discovered something we all have—little pleasure centers in the brain. The unusually large human brain got that way only because it provided us with some advantage. That advantage is the ability to figure things out, something that our nonhuman competitors, so far as we know, are not very good at. Using the brain to do what it evolved to do provides a bit of satisfaction so that we will be encouraged to use it that way again. After all, what good is a big brain if it isn't used? We find evidence for this in the little kick we get from solving a puzzle or the aptly named "brain teaser." Fortunate are those students who discover that learning new things tickles the brain. Actually, *rediscover* would be a better word. When we were children, we all wanted to do things for ourselves and find out about our world. College is seen in a new way when it becomes an occasion for stimulating the brain and rediscovering those forgotten pleasure centers.

Is It Worth the Effort?

The alert reader will have noticed that there have been no sections called "Note-Taking Made Easy" or "Four Easy Steps for Improving Reading Skills." There's good reason. You would be suspicious if a weight training book had a section called "Bench-Pressing 300 Pounds Made Easy," or a piano book had a chapter titled "Beethoven Sonatas Made Easy." The belief that learning can be made easy springs from the mistaken notion that learning is somehow not a physical process. We assume the ice skater's triple jumps are difficult *because* they are so physical: they require practiced coordination and developed muscle strength and tone. We know that physical strength and coordination come only with doing. You learn to ski by skiing, not by reading about it. The only secret is practice. But learning is also a physical process, and only practice will improve it.

Learning involves the brain, an organ every bit as physical as the biceps. Both muscle and brain are changed by use. The idea that learning changes the brain the way exercise changes the muscles frightens some people. Doing things to the brain sounds spooky—better to leave well enough alone. We would never think like that if our muscles were involved. We know they get better with use. If we don't use them, they will literally shrink and weaken. The brain is definitely not a muscle, but it *is* a physical organ. It does develop through use, and development implies some change. Putting the brain through its paces is going to require an expenditure of energy as surely as does lifting weights. Be wary of anyone who claims that it can be made easy.

If we are to work at something—burn a little energy—we have a right to expect a return on the investment. No one would lift weights week after week for years if they never got any stronger or their muscles never got any larger. Nor would anyone practice the piano hour upon hour if their playing never improved. Where, then, is the return on the investment of energy that goes into learning?

As surely as the practiced gymnast achieves a nimble body, the practiced learner develops a nimble mind. Furthermore, nothing about humans stays in good condition as long as the mind. A quick and agile mind will serve you long after the muscles have slowed down. Even so, the curiosity that prompts the need to know, and so learning, needs to be indulged early. The curiosity you had as a child may have been dulled through a long association of learning with the storing of a lot of facts in short-term memory. College is the perfect time to reinvigorate your curiosity—to wonder again about how things work and how they got to be the way they are.

Will discovering and indulging a need to know really have an effect? Does it guarantee anything more than grades? It will if you are ready to accept real change. Shelby Steele has remarked that the reason we come to college is to be remade. Probably not many of us started out with that purpose, but there are some who do discover it early on, and there are many more who could. Whoever truly learns is changed by the process. Figuring out relations, causes and effects, consequences, conclusions, and implications, and formulating all that into proper language is going to leaves tracks in the brain. People who store things often have difficulty recalling them. Those who learn things have a hard time forgetting them.

three

Teachers

Student Voices

MY PHYSICS PROFESSOR IS A DIFFERENT PERSON OUT-
SIDE CLASS. HE REMINDS ME OF MY UNCLE GEORGE.
HE'S REALLY EASY TO TALK TO.

— GERRY

mid the excitement of getting started in September, you may be on campus some time before encountering a teacher. In some schools, they tend to drift onto the scene after orientation, registration, book buying, the rock concert, and after the uproar has subsided. For all their quiet entrance, they're going to have an impact on your academic life. A few might well influence the course of your life for many years to come. Such things don't just happen, however. Just as the success of your academic life will be determined by your attitude toward learning, the help teachers can provide will be determined in large part by your attitude toward them.

Anyone who talks about teachers is tempted to make grand general statements: "They all . . . ." In reality, there are few general statements about teachers that are both useful and true. One thing you can be reasonably sure of is that they are well versed in the subject areas they teach. Unless your instructor is a TA (teaching assistant: a graduate student studying for a higher degree), she very likely has an advanced degree in her subject area. Advanced degrees are awarded by scholars to certify that someone has met certain standards of learning and research in their field of specialization.

Nor will you find an economics professor taking over a course in political science or a mathematician teaching physics. Colleges are quite fussy about such things. Your teachers will have spent many years seriously studying the subjects they teach.

Beyond that, few generalizations will hold up. While most teachers I know like what they do, a few are indeed grumpy. Most of them like the students they teach, but now and again you find an unpleasant one. Even in the area of concern here—what and how students learn—a few are content if students simply remember the words they intone or recognize related items on a multiple-choice test. At most colleges, though, most of your teachers will see themselves more as guides in your overall education than as mere dispensers of information. They will take some personal responsibility in your intellectual development. Still, even in the most prestigious institutions there will be a few who merely deliver the facts of their discipline. They lecture; the rest is up to you. At a more personal level, most teachers will treat college students as adults, but there will be a few who interact with students as if they were children. In short, teachers, like the members of any other profession, are a mixed bag.

False Impressions

A frequent first impression of college is that it is impersonal: less friendly than high school, including the teachers. The college format contributes to that impression. Some freshman classes have hundreds of students: someone in the back row wouldn't even recognize the teacher if they passed him on the street; the teacher, in turn, doesn't seem too concerned as to whether students even show up or not. Your class in history may meet in the engineering building and you don't recognize anyone. The teacher comes in from the other side of campus, shaking the rain from his coat. His mind is on history and he starts right in. You may well find yourself longing for the days when you stayed in the same building all day, everyone knew everyone else, and the teachers all knew your name.

In truth, most teachers don't like the typical arrangement any more than the students do. We would all like to have small classes, where we knew everyone's name, and in rooms of our own choosing. But even in a less than ideal environment, teachers can teach and students can learn. More serious than a cold or impersonal room is the feeling that the instructor is cold and impersonal. In fact, college teachers, as a group, are probably more friendly and approachable than most. You will see shortly how to prove this to yourself.

What Do Teachers Want?

C ollege teaching does not involve quite as many specific "do this, do that" instructions as you may be accustomed to. Things seem a little loose; new students sometimes have difficulty nailing down just what their teachers expect. The concern here is not so much with the quantitative aspects of college learning—how many books have to be read or how long the reports must be—but with the expectations of teachers who want learning that goes deeper than the facts, beyond recall and recognition. If you find a teacher who always seems to want something more of you, you will have stumbled onto someone who has the potential for making a difference in your life.

You can identify such teachers by being alert to certain telltale signs. Look for teachers who engage students in conversation, or even debate. Listen for the hypothetical question "Yes, but what if...?" Teachers who are trying to lead you into the world of the mind are difficult to satisfy. They are interested not only in your answers, but in how you arrived at them. Nothing ever seems quite enough. How did these people get that way? Why do they constantly push students?

All of your teachers have spent many years in school. First they were undergraduates, as you are now; then they were graduate students, perhaps postdoctoral scholars; some of them may have been in college classrooms for the past forty or fifty years. They are dedicated people who did not quit learning at the end of graduate school. Most college teachers continue doing research in their areas of interest for many years. They write books, compose music, paint, discover new truths, write articles in scholarly journals, and continue learning about things that are dear to them for as long as they are healthy. What most discover over the years is that the learning they do later in life is different from that of their undergraduate days. Once they are no longer going to class themselves, they find that they are not dependent on teachers. No one gives them a reading list or assigns writing that they must turn in on a certain date. They are on their own.

College teachers do not believe that their jobs involve nothing more than teaching what they learned when they were students. They must continue to learn as well as to teach, but their learning is now self-motivated. They have experienced the need to know, and now, on their own, they are driven to learn as much as they can. They might scan twenty to thirty articles a week, not to store all that in their memory, but to evaluate—to determine whether the information is really new, important, and likely to be true. They might read twenty, thirty, or forty books a year—again, not with the expectation of retaining everything, but to keep abreast of current thinking and new developments. They may abandon some books after reading a few pages; others will be pored over and annotated and will make major contributions to their thinking. They are continually evaluating and learning, and they find it enormously satisfying.

Many of us find this kind of learning far superior to that of our early years as students. Some of us were not particularly good students during those years. We did what we were told and hoped for the best. But if we were lucky, we had a few teachers who were not content with reciting their discipline, but questioned us, inspired us, and showed us that we could learn something in depth. Most of us who have the desire to become lifelong learners can trace it to these teachers and to the goals they set for us. This new kind of learning, which satisfies our curiosity and drives us to learn more, is so superior that we want the same for our students.

You may well ask, "Wouldn't it be far easier to avoid such people altogether?" Of course it would be easier—just as it is easier not to lift weights, not to practice your backhand, not to do gymnastics, not to play scales. Doing only what is easy, however, will mean never being really good at anything. No one who wanted to excel in some area would turn down the opportunity to work with an acknowledged master. To avoid the best teachers in college is to miss the point of why you came here in the first place.

The New Environment

Teachers who want to raise you to a new level of knowing and thinking are just one part, but a most significant part, of a larger pattern of change that characterizes the sudden transition to college life. The problems associated with living away from home, or commuting, or the loose, rambling nature of a college campus—and that double-edged sword, freedom—are well known and have been thoroughly discussed in other books. However, it is not always recognized that your encounters with teachers who expect thinking and learning in a new way make up one of the most important parts of that transition.

If it is true, as Shelby Steele said, that we come to college to remake ourselves, then serious change cannot be avoided. Change considered in an abstract way—realizing vaguely that we will continue to get older, will take jobs, will have children, and so on—does not upset most people. That kind of change is felt to be out there somewhere, waiting to happen to us as the tide of life carries us along. But when someone is told that over the next several years their taste in music might change radically, or that they will change their political views, or the people they want to have as friends, they tend to get nervous. Even if we admit that we have gone through such changes in the past, the prospect of future changes in our thinking—particularly if they should result in new behaviors—makes us wary.

A significant area of possible change, and one that involves teachers prominently, is the way we interact with people, particularly those who are older or who in some way represent authority figures. The so-called traditional new college student—eighteen or nineteen years old—has just left an environment that changed little over the course of four years. The group that graduated from high school was roughly the same group that had entered four years earlier; seldom does the building change much, and there is rarely a big turnover of teachers. So while young people are changing from fourteen-year-olds to eighteen-year-olds, their environment remains substantially the same. One result is that the people in such a situation, both students and teachers (sometimes parents) may get stuck in behavior patterns that are no longer appropriate. High school teachers see fourteen-year-old freshmen as large, rambunctious children and react appropriately, applying restraints and rules. High school freshmen respond appropriately, and quickly determine which rules and which enforcers are serious. Whether the rules and their enforcers are lenient or lax is not the question. The point is that high school is rule-oriented and re-inforces the adult/child relationship between teachers and students. Teachers make rules and students obey to the extent the rules are enforced. This adult/child relationship between teachers and students tends not to change substantially over a four-year period, even though the student becomes four years older. And so the traditional freshman often comes to college with a child-to-adult mindset with respect to teachers. We need, then, to take a closer look at the environment the new college student is entering in order to understand why this mindset makes the transition needlessly perplexing.

The vast majority of college teachers do not have experience teaching fourteen-year-olds. They long ago worked their way through the transition, and are into adult/adult relationships almost exclusively (except possibly for their own children). The psychologist Eric Berne has shown that child/adult relationships work fine so long as both parties know their own roles in the re-lationship. So long as one party sees herself as adult and the other as child, and the second party sees himself as child and the other as adult, things will go well. Trouble begins when the two perceive the relationship differently. This is precisely what happens in the case of many new college students. Most college teachers consider college freshmen to be adults and they behave ap-propriately as adult to adult. Far too many new students are still stuck in the child/adult relationship with respect to teachers. Misunderstanding is almost inevitable.

Adult/Adult Relations

Perhaps it should be made clear at this point that not every teacher you encounter is going to fit the picture I have been painting. As I've hinted above, some may not even like teaching at all, but consider it a necessary evil that comes with their own ongoing learning and development. Some may merely lecture you with little concern about your learning; a few may even treat you as a child. What really concerns us here are those who do like teach-ing, do like students, and are quite concerned with furthering your intellectual life, but are misunderstood because their behavior is unfamiliar.

What's unfamiliar is the adult/adult attitude. This may sound strange in-deed to someone who is quite tired of being treated like a child. It also brings up a strange-sounding but serious question: How do you know when you're being treated as an adult?

This is not the place to discuss all the details of adult/adult relations, but there are a few aspects of such relations that affect new college students partic-ularly. Notably, a mature adult, at least one who does not want to be consid-ered a busybody, does not intrude uninvited into the life of another adult. This includes refraining from offering unsolicited advice. A mature adult is honest with others and expects the same in return. He is willing to admit at least the possibility that another's opinion might be as valid as his own. He accepts the consequences of his free actions. A mature adult is not inherently suspicious of other adults.

Clearly I have presented an idealized case. Not all adults have the traits I've described simply because they have gotten older. The point is that new students, when they do encounter such mature behavior in a teacher, can find it confusing. The teacher, for example, who never asks why a student missed class or failed to turn in an assignment might be considered either a little dotty or simply not much interested in students at all. If such teachers accept, a time or two at least, totally outrageous excuses for missing an exam, they might be thought of as "easy." If they announce that submitted assignments are a requirement for passing and do indeed give failing grades to students who don't do the assignments, they are sometimes said to be unfair.

Being treated in these ways is not what a child has come to expect. An essential element of normal, healthy childhood is having an adult around to set the rules, impose discipline, and, when all else fails, clean up afterward. During the transition phase, we would like to pick and choose our adult behaviors. We would prefer to make our own rules and get free of the discipline, but it would be terrifically comforting if we could still have someone to bail us out of jams. The problem with college is that these adult/adult interactions come all at once. Almost overnight, the rules change and we find that we can pick our own schedule, choose among teachers, skip class, miss the due dates, or sleep through a morning exam without anyone yelling at us or laying down the law. But neither will anyone spare us the consequences of those actions. Most of your teachers, following the adult/adult rules, will assume that you are capable of handling your own affairs and would ask for advice if you needed it. It is sad to see a freshman misunderstand what is going on, make a shambles of the first year, and offer as explanation the perception that "no one here cares." In such a case, adult behavior is being misinterpreted as lack of concern.

Clearly, when I talk of such misunderstanding, I do not have all college freshmen in mind. Some eighteen-year-olds are ready for, and welcome, what Jacques Barzun calls "the first mature interplay of minds." But even those who are ready for it do not always know how to recognize it. An adult treating you like an adult is not the same as a friendly and concerned adult treating you like a loved child.

One of the reasons I believe that the adult/adult relationship contributes to the transition problem derives from the observation that older beginning students have fewer problems with this aspect of college life. Someone who has been out of school for some years comes to college experienced in adult/adult relations. They tend to understand their teachers better, even if they also struggle with the new expectations of learning in depth.

The absence of continual supervision and monitoring by teachers is, I believe, the aspect of adult behavior that most confuses new students. Teachers who do not advise students that they have missed assignments or quizzes, or that their performance is not up to par, are seen by some students as indifferent or unconcerned. Quite simply, this is not a valid conclusion. The Harvard Assessment Seminars Report details careful studies that were carried out to determine whether students felt that college teachers, especially the more prestigious ones, were indifferent, aloof, and inaccessible. Upper-division students and graduates were quite insistent that this was not the case. What these more experienced students noted was that the great majority of their teachers kept their office hours and welcomed students who dropped by for a chat or coffee.

However, two aspects of these faculty/student interactions should be emphasized. In the first instance, the teachers made themselves available and were receptive to discussions, but did not initiate contact themselves. Students who took the initiative were generally rewarded with a friendly reception and a productive interchange of ideas. Taking the initiative is, however, an adult-type behavior that does not come easily until it is practiced. Second, the content of faculty/student discussion had to stay on an adult level. Discussions—even arguments—about theories, solutions to problems, or books and authors were always welcome. Anything like whining—to the effect, say, that the teacher's course was ruining the student's grade point average—was not well received. This difference speaks directly to the heart of the adult/adult relation.

A teacher who engages a student in debate about some fact or theory is demonstrating an adult characteristic that I spoke of earlier: the assumption that someone else may have a valid opinion or possess useful facts. She is also educating in the best sense, by encouraging the verbalization of ideas. That same teacher is likely to be impatient with the student who comes to explain that his absence from an exam was excusable because it came on the last day before spring break and everyone knows students leave early for spring break. Lack of sympathy in this case derives from another characteristic of adult behavior: An action taken freely implies acceptance of its consequences. For a child, parents and teachers often make allowances and, when possible, compensate for or negate the consequences of impulsive behavior. It's a hard lesson indeed when this comfortable arrangement comes, at last, to an end, but responsibility is the price of liberty.

Teachers in the Classroom

Puzzling or unfamiliar behavior on the part of teachers will most likely be first encountered in the classroom. College teachers of the type I have been describing might be said to be in the grip of the material they teach. Some seem so absorbed that you feel they would go on talking even if everyone slipped out the back. Others are student-conscious, but show it by pestering you with questions when you would like nothing better than to rest undisturbed. Many will not organize material for you, but simply discourse (which often sounds like rambling to a new student). A history teacher, caught up in the drama of unfolding events, may relate a long, involved story, dropping dates and names casually and giving no indication of one thing being more important than another. This kind of teacher puts pressure on new students to listen with unaccustomed attentiveness and to do their own organizing, which is often expected to be completed outside the classroom. Some teachers never take roll. Some pass out a syllabus with dates for exam periods and assignments, and never mention it again until the due dates arrive. It is easy to get the impression that some of these teachers are not concerned with you and the difficulties their course may be causing.

Coping with the college classroom will be taken up later. My intent here is to concentrate more on the teachers involved and to show how adult/adult behavior can be misinterpreted. Most teachers will assume, for example, that adults who pay money to attend lectures on history or economics are interested in learning something about those subjects. They would find it puzzling that a student would enroll in a course with no other goal than getting credits to go on her transcript. And so they treat the class as a group of adults interested in learning. Few college instructors believe it is possible to help someone who doesn't want to learn. So if they don't threaten, or chase after you for assignments, it's not that they don't care; it's just not the way adults treat other adults.

Such teachers may do other puzzling things. They sometimes assign a book or chapter and never mention it again or question you on it. You might easily assume that the teacher simply wasn't serious and the reading wasn't really important. The teacher, on the other hand, may be thinking that if no one raises a question or makes a comment, then everyone has done the reading and has had no problem with it. Dozens of such illustrations are possible, but the central idea, again, is that the teacher is making two assumptions about adult behavior: Students want to learn, and they will speak up when they are having difficulties.

Outside the Classroom

For some students, the teacher ceases to exist outside the classroom. This is indeed unfortunate, even unnatural in light of our ordinary behavior. People tend to bump into one another, exchange pleasantries, visit, have coffee, exchange ideas or opinions, or ask for information or advice. In truth, it takes some students a while to begin thinking of teachers as people in this sense. One such young man, visiting a local watering hole on a Friday afternoon, was surprised to discover several teachers and a clutch of students engaged in lively debate over who was more responsible for a host of evils, the scientists who create technology or the businessmen who make and sell it. He got no answer to that enduring question, but he did get a glimpse of young people enjoying their first "interplay of mature minds." He thought it was a terrific new idea, even though it's as old as Socrates.

Students in general tend to enjoy and profit from interchanges with teachers that take place outside a classroom. Many, unfortunately, still assume that any such encounters must be, or should be, initiated and organized by the teacher. But as we've seen, most teachers do not see students as children to be taken care of. Students are considered to be adults who will speak up when there is a need. Students, too often, interpret their teachers' reluctance to interfere as indifference. The solution to this problem is simple: Make the first move. It's the adult thing to do.

The most common nonclassroom interaction between students and teachers is the one-to-one conversation, before or after a class or in the teacher's office. Even here, far too many students appear to consider such conversations to be in some way out of the ordinary. The assumption seems to be that you need a special and pressing reason to interrupt a teacher's busy life with talk. This is seldom the case. True, a few teachers might consider themselves too important to take time for undergraduates, but you probably wouldn't want to talk with them anyway. Most teachers respond happily to a request for a few minutes' time.

There are several easy ways to initiate a conversation. None of them is in any way unusual, nor will any of them cause the teacher to consider you peculiar. The brief period after class is usually a good time either to spend a few minutes on something that was not clear, or to arrange for a short talk in the teacher's office. Few teachers object to a walking companion on the way to the next class or to the office. A simple "Hi" usually gets a friendly response. Identify yourself, if that is necessary, and talk about whatever it is you think this person might have a good idea about. There are also office hours. Virtually all colleges insist that teachers who instruct undergraduates set aside fixed periods, usually several hours each week, during which the teacher is available to students. Usually appointments are not necessary during office hours, but check just in case. It is not at all necessary to have a "serious" reason for talking with teachers. In fact, if you wait until things become serious, you may have waited too long.

There is a certain etiquette that shapes these adult/adult interactions. It is not a good idea, for example, to go to a teacher's office with the request that she repeat yesterday's lecture for you because your alarm did not go off. The most congenial people I know are both irritated and offended by such requests. Had you found out on your own the topics covered, read the relevant material, discussed it with a classmate, and finally come in to clear up a few remaining problems, you would most likely receive a friendly welcome and the help you need. The first case suggests a child asking an adult to straighten out the mess he's made. The second is one adult getting help from another.

A Paradox

A paradox is a situation that appears self-contradictory, but is nonetheless true. The paradox in the present case is that those teachers with the greatest potential for helping in your intellectual development can cause the most problems early on. We have seen that there are reasons for this. Good teachers may frustrate new students because they are not satisfied with recall and recognition learning. They want something more for their students. They want their students to learn the way they do, to satisfy a deep need to know. However, they know that such a method cannot be explained; it can only be experienced. Their attempts to inculcate habits of the mind can be quite bewildering to the new student. Should a student continue to approach these teachers in the child/adult mode, and these teachers reject that kind of relationship, then the situation becomes doubly perplexing.

I am reminded here of an elderly and very refined professor from my own college days. After a particularly involved proof or refutation, he would turn from the board with a flourish and pace, quietly and with long stately strides, up and down the aisles while we pondered. He would stop suddenly next to some student, address him by name, and ask, "Am I bothering you?" It was a soft and gentle voice without a trace of sarcasm. We soon learned the dangers of answering "No." Not to be bothered was to understand completely, and so we would be asked to repeat the proof. He believed that an unbothered student either was not being sufficiently challenged or was simply not learning anything. Most of us were bothered most of the time.

I started to enter the classroom one day, only to find that same gentleman blocking my way with his hands on his hips. He stared down at me and growled, "*You.*" He then pulled me aside and rehearsed in remarkable detail some astoundingly foolish thing I had written on the last exam. I still remember walking away from that tongue-lashing quite exhilarated and in good humor. He was the first person to ever show real concern as to whether or not I was learning anything.

New Beginnings

It might be said that teachers are not paid to educate, but to teach. Education is what students do to themselves; teachers are the guides and coaches. In a certain sense, they are there to be used. Pursuing teachers and picking their brains is what it's all about. Such behavior seldom comes naturally to new students, however. Becoming friends with a teacher or showing a serious interest in learning can be a source of ridicule in high school; fear of that ridicule may have to be unlearned.

It is just here that the radically new environment of college can be a real blessing. Some people persist for years in inappropriate behavior, for no other reason than that their family and friends have come to expect it. They are trapped in their environment and their actions dictated by it. College offers an opportunity for a fresh start. Many students show up on campus knowing absolutely no one. The plus side is that absolutely no one knows them either. Anyone looking for an opportunity to change his lifestyle, without alarming his friends, will find no better place than college. One young man, in a moment of endearing honesty, told me that starting college was the greatest thing ever to happen to him—because at last he could quit acting like a juvenile.

Teachers in particular are not going to be surprised by sudden changes in your attitude or behavior. They never knew you before either. To them, nothing could be more welcome than a new student eager to learn about the things they know best.

College can be defined in a number of ways, but for the new student it is best thought of as a collection of experts, brought together for the express purpose of putting you through the wringer—taking your mind as far as it can go. *Carpe diem*: Seize the day.

four

Attending Class

Student Voices

WHAT'S THE POINT OF GOING TO CLASS? ALL HE DOES IS
TALK. I HAVEN'T TAKEN A SINGLE NOTE!

—MICHELLE

 et's assume you now believe that college is going to be quite different from anything that came before. Quite often your teachers will expect a different kind of learning and they're going to treat you pretty much as an adult. We come, then, to what most students consider the essential activity: going to classes. Whatever is said here about going to classes is intended to apply to laboratories, studios, and recitations as well as lectures. (*Lecture*, though it is an old-fashioned word, is still widely used to indicate the two, three, or more periods each week when teachers and students meet in classrooms.)

Attitudes

The way you start any new endeavor is much determined by the attitude you bring to it. It is often possible to change attitudes in mid-course, but in the case we will be considering now—attending classes—getting a good start is very important. The images or ideas that appear in your head when you hear the word *attend*, for example, are clues to your present attitude. The word *attend* has about seven meanings. One meaning is *to be present*; another meaning is *to be attentive to*. What you get from lectures will very much depend on which meaning applies to you. Do you intend to just be present while the teacher earns her living, or to be attentive to what is going on?

There is also the problem of the self-fulfilling prophecy, which in this case means that you are likely to have a pre-formed notion of what the lecture is supposed to do, and that notion determines what you do during the lecture, which in turn will cause your expectation to come true. All of which means you had better have the correct expectations right from the start. Let's first consider two "wrong" expectations.

1. "The lecture is that period in which the teacher outlines what is to be learned later." Sounds good, but it isn't. Few teachers see this as their task, and few conduct their courses this way.

2. "Attending class is what I have to do to get credit." This is worse yet. It suggests again that the student views the college experience as a kind of contract, whereby a diploma is awarded if certain tasks are carried out and certain rules are followed. In fact, that is precisely true, but getting the diploma is not the same as getting an education.

This second point was illustrated clearly some years ago, when a parent sued a college because it had given a diploma to his son, who was, in fact, every bit as ignorant after college as he had been before. The parent saw it as a clear case of breach of contract. He confused a diploma with an education. The diploma certifies only that a student has been given every opportunity to educate himself. The lecture is one such opportunity. To approach it as a duty, or as part of a bargain, or as that time of day when the teacher, by way of notes, provides clues to exam questions, is to waste a marvelous opportunity.

Experienced students have come to recognize that the well-prepared and well-presented lecture can become a period of concentrated study. They also know that learning is not an automatic consequence of attending and does not depend primarily on the teacher. The format of the lecture is determined by the instructor; what is learned is determined by the student. The teacher is a resource, a guide, and a coach. Few college teachers "teach to the test," meaning they use the lecture to preview what will appear on the exams. Some teachers are not even very interesting to listen to. In short, the lecture can be a highly efficient learning period, but not if you depend on the teacher to do all the work.

Behind these comments lies the assumption that the student does indeed have the desire to learn in depth. When a course is not of your own choosing—a science course for the literature major, or German for the chemistry major—it is terribly tempting to approach it as something to be endured. You can, however, with a small adjustment of attitude, see any course as an opportunity. What possible harm could come from learning German, for example, or from discovering how scientists arrive at their theories and laws? How many people wish they had the opportunity! Seeing the lecture as opportunity rather than obligation can effect significant changes in what you do before, during, and after class.

Work for the Mind

For you to learn during the lecture, a clear requirement is that the mind be engaged. You cannot learn passively; watching what goes on, or even being entertained by it, will not do anything for your mind. Attending lectures, in the sense of being present, will not result in education. An active mind is a necessary condition. That claim rests on good data. Physiologists have shown that in subjects who are absorbed in some problem, calculating or trying to figure out some puzzle, the metabolic activity in certain regions of the brain is increased to an extent that is detectable by electronic equipment. When the same subjects are engaged in matching words or copying lists of items, their brains calm down and appear to "go on standby."

Activity that does not increase brain metabolism is not making any changes there. Learning in depth requires changes that leave tracks in the brain. Furthermore, the regions of the brain that burn calories during concentrated learning are not the same ones we use for seeing or hearing in the purely physical sense. What these complicated biological facts tell us is that you can watch and hear what is happening in class without ever turning on that part of the brain where learning goes on. If the lecture period is not to be wasted, the mind must become engaged.

To learn, we must intend to learn. Making good use of the lecture is an example of a general rule: Never assume that physical activities alone—showing up, seeing, hearing, without intent and decision—will do the job of learning. No matter how religiously followed, no "technique" will produce serious learning unless the mind is truly involved. In fact, someone with a burning curiosity and a need to know will find a way to learn, whether he knows "techniques" or not. This book will indeed present things you can do to improve your ability to learn in depth, but always with the assumption that you intend to learn: to engage the mind and get the brain working.

Go In Prepared

So what do you do during the lectures of one of those instructors who is "into deep learning" and has no patience with reciting the textbook? First, find out what that teacher expects in the way of preparation. Ideally, preparing means both reviewing and looking ahead, but the emphasis will change from class to class. In the sciences, you will certainly be expected to have learned or reviewed what went on previously. Scientific knowledge builds on prior knowledge and understanding. Science teachers seldom expect you to have already learned on your own what they are about to present, but you are definitely expected to understand and remember what has already been presented so that you'll be ready for the new material. In the humanities, it is frequently the opposite. You cannot appreciate a lecture analyzing the style of a story, or contribute intelligently to a discussion of that story, if you haven't read it. Unless specifically told to do otherwise, use the following general rule: In the sciences, prepare for the lecture by reviewing; in the humanities, read ahead.

Preparing also means getting the right mindset for what's about to happen. It's not a good idea to enter the classroom as an observer. To see the teacher as performer—earning her pay by putting on a show—and the class as audience, is to shift the burden again. The work of education, from this point of view, is transferred from student to teacher. Think instead of the teacher as someone who has what you came to college to find. The lecture is the time you are allotted to find out what he knows, to pick his brain, and to find out whether your understanding of things is logical, consistent, and true.

Making Notes

Few things are more quickly picked up by new students than the impression that teachers talk, or show slides, or write on the board, and students write in notebooks. How thoroughly ingrained this belief can become is illustrated by the young woman who, having been absent from a lecture, asked the teacher, "Did I miss anything yesterday? Like, did you give notes?" The teacher spent the rest of the day in a blue funk. He had envisioned himself as coach and guide, leading young minds toward greater things; the student saw him as a dispenser of notes.

The notion that the lecture period is a time set aside for the giving and taking of notes will cause enormous mischief. If this giving and taking were the point of college, we could easily save the expense of building lecture halls and classrooms. Teachers could supply "notes" on floppy disks. Students could copy these with a keystroke and have a flawless version of the teacher's notes. The fault in that scheme is obvious: It can all be done without mental activity.

We are mistaken again if we believe that the hearing of the teacher's words and the physical writing of notes guarantee that the learning part of the brain is engaged. That this is not the case is illustrated by those expert secretaries who can take minutes at a meeting, make an excellent transcript of nearly everything said, and not remember a word of it—or even, in some cases, understand what was said. There is a potent lesson here. Hearing, seeing, and writing all involve different parts of the brain from those used for thinking and understanding. We can sometimes feel something like a switch go on in our heads when we need to think carefully about something. Consider the following parable, which illustrates the point:

Someone tells you that he is about to recite from memory some complicated instructions as to how to find a box hidden in a certain part of the city. If you can follow these instructions and find the box, you can have it and its contents. The box contains $100,000. One hundred thousand dollars, there for the taking, tends to focus the attention. We feel something click in the brain; understanding the upcoming instructions becomes a driving need. Would you merely listen to the words without taking notes? Would you only hope that you could remember street names, numbers, distances, and descriptions? Would you be content with "doing the best you can?" Would you trust that the information would come to you when you needed it?

More likely, you would process every last detail in your own mind and use your mental picture to draw a map. It would be labeled in complete detail, street names spelled correctly, numbers checked and rechecked. You would instantly reread the notes you took to see that nothing had been left out. You wouldn't let your benefactor get away until every question had been answered and the path to the money was absolutely clear in your mind *and* on paper.

The intent here is not to suggest that introductory sociology will be or can be as riveting as a box full of money. The story only shows what the mind is capable of; it illustrates what all of us can and would do when we absolutely must understand.

In order to understand the importance of being mentally engaged while listening and writing in class, think of notes as something you *make* rather than something you *take*. *Taking* has that feel of receiving what has been given. It suggests passive acceptance—a mechanical transfer. To *make* a note implies that the mental activity involved occurs in the mind of the note maker. Mental activity is the goal here. How, then, does one make notes?

Note making implies going beyond transcribing what is said or written. That does not mean, however, that transcribing is to be disdained, that it is of no use. Certainly, if a teacher has done you the favor of generating an outline of upcoming events, or a summary of major ideas, it would be foolish not to use that information and include it in your notes. The trouble frequently starts when the teacher finishes the outline, or steps away from the board, and begins talking. As I suggested earlier, very few teachers read to students from notes or from a text. They come prepared with certain ideas they want to discuss, but not with the words they will use. They generate the language on the run, so to speak, and what they actually say often sounds casual and conversational. It would because they are creating sentences as needed. It is just here that the inexperienced or unwary will be tempted to put down the pencil, get comfortable, and listen to the story—or tune out and daydream.

Teachers who are just talking, particularly in a relaxed and apparently less organized way, are seen by some as no longer *giving notes*. And what is not given cannot be taken. But it is just here that we must change our way of thinking about the lecture, and about our part in it. A teacher who does provide an outline of the important ideas in that day's lecture is very likely to then discourse, less formally, on the importance of what has been outlined. The causes of events, or their significance, or the evidence for theories, might be presented from memory by way of anecdote, research experience, or paraphrases of many dozens of books and articles. When such discourses are presented in an engaging style, students characterize the teacher as "interesting." Do be careful when you encounter "interesting" teachers. They can make an hour zip by, and at the end you may very well find in your notebook nothing but the names of a few organs and enzymes or a list of names and dates. At a later time, you will likely become aware—and painfully so—that what you were really expected to learn was the significance or the history of the items in the outline, or the evidence for the claims that were made. And all that vital information was in the storytelling part of the lecture, the part that never was written on the blackboard or shown in a slide.

Many new students, if not a majority, get caught off base in those courses where the teachers do not provide detailed line-by-line notes of everything the student is expected to know. You will do well to learn quickly how to cope. The short answer is to make your own notes in those courses. How you do this is the crux of the problem. If a teacher is indeed interesting, you will likely hear everything that is said. But hearing, you will remember, does not take place in the thinking part of the brain. Hearing becomes *listening* only when the meanings of words and sentences rumble around in the thinking part of the brain and become ideas. *Hearing* means being aware of what was said. *Listening* means thinking what the speaker is thinking. When the teacher's thoughts become your thoughts, you may find yourself suddenly realizing, "Wow, she just told us how this whole thing works and I haven't written a word!" I hope for you that this revelation comes early, because it means that you will soon be listening, extracting what's explanatory, and writing, preferably in words of your own, notes on those interesting (and critically important) discourses and musings. Extracting the meaning and writing it—using your own vocabulary—is known as paraphrasing: an idea of great importance that will come up again.

This, in short, is what I mean by *making notes*. Nearly all seniors have learned to do it. They can be seen writing furiously while the teacher stands looking out the window, more or less thinking out loud. Four years earlier, they would more likely have sat staring at the teacher, waiting for something to happen. There is no reason to learn this lesson the hard way, through repeated experiences. Beginning students who set their minds to it can make good notes almost from the beginning. You will get better and better with practice, however.

Note making, then, brings together several of the requirements for serious learning. It cannot be done passively; learning students work harder during the lecture than the teacher does. It presumes a need to know what the teacher finds important and interesting. Finally, it absolutely requires that the thinking part of the brain be actively engaged.

Participate

Being called on to recite in class is the third most frequent dream, after snakes and spiders, that brings parents running to children's bedrooms in the middle of the night. No matter how that phobia got started, it does hang on. More than a few college students will drop a course the same day they learn that they will be expected to recite or to participate in discussions. I have great empathy with people who are asked to face up to what they dread most. But some fears are realistic and others spring entirely from an imagined evil. Truly, for some people, having public attention focused on them is the most unbearable thing they can imagine. Still, despite talk to the contrary, no death certificate has ever listed acute embarrassment as the cause of death. You can ruin your life if you devote it to avoiding every possible occasion of embarrassment. Better by far to get a grip on the cause of the embarrassment and try to fix that.

The panic that seems to grip us by the throat when a teacher asks us to say something probably had its origin in our early schooling. When we were small, adults were by nature intimidating, and teachers particularly so. Then there was the "right answer" we were always expected to recall instantly. Intimidating teachers and "right answers" are still found, here and there, at the college level. Many of your teachers, on the other hand, are only trying to get you to do the verbalizing I mentioned earlier. They want you to put thought into words because that process both demonstrates and causes learning. Some of your teachers will also be teaching upper-division classes, where students might be quite uninhibited. Such teachers are probably accustomed to being questioned, or asked for clarification or examples, or even challenged if they accidentally (or intentionally) say something outrageous. It's that "mature interplay of minds" I discussed earlier, and most teachers love it. They may come into a freshman class and try to get the same sort of thing going. Go along with it! Speaking in class loses its terror when it is perceived as a simple matter of two adults talking to one another.

One would like, nevertheless, to have something sensible to say should the occasion arise. When you learn to make your own notes on the lecture, having something to say is not such a big problem. If you're thinking right along with the teacher, her request for an answer or comment will not come like a bolt out of the blue. Surely the topic must be the very thing you were hearing and thinking about. Responding is beneficial to you because it provides practice verbalizing. Don't spoil the opportunity by giving a one-word answer. Be bold and uncork something like a sentence. One-word answers, or "I don't know," are disheartening to the teacher, and they do not constitute verbalizing, which is the intent of it all. There's nothing wrong with starting a response by saying, "It could be that...," or "Is that a case in which...." Teachers who ask for a response from a student are not necessarily "testing" the student. Just as likely, they are looking for evidence that the student is thinking about the problem at hand.

Teachers nearly always welcome questions, provided a certain etiquette is observed. "Is this going to be on the test?" is a question that, frankly, has no place in the college classroom. "You've lost me" is likewise not very helpful. It sounds more like an accusation than a question. But there are occasions when, in spite of your best efforts, things simply go too fast. Some teachers believe, mistakenly, that quiet in the classroom signifies that everyone has understood every word. You will help yourself and everyone else by calling a little time out when you're doing your best and still find yourself lost. Again, a kind of protocol must be followed here. Try to find the exact cause of confusion; be as specific as you can. "When X happens, does that mean…" is the type of question that suggests an alert student who has become momentarily lost. "I don't understand any of this," on the other hand, suggests that the teacher has made a bad job of it. Nothing is gained by irritating the teacher.

Thinking along with the teacher, making your own notes, and not letting confusing things go by, all contribute to making the lecture what it should be, a period of concentrated learning. Few of us see lectures in this way at the beginning. The lecture, particularly when the teacher is a fast talker, can become a period of writing down as much as you can, thinking you can worry about it later. This is not good strategy. Words that made no sense when you wrote them will not become magically clear days or weeks later. Those pages of confusing words and disconnected phrases will begin piling up. In desperation, you'll resort to memorizing lists and diagrams. If you do keep up by using time between classes to stay abreast, using the text or assigned readings, you are still adding unnecessarily to the time spent on each course.

Consider the woman who returned to college while raising a family and working part-time. It was impossible for her to study at home, and after attending classes she had very few hours in the week when she could go to the library and read undisturbed. She maintained a B+ average only because she had discovered that she could learn during the lecture. She always reviewed the previous class, even if only during the five or ten minutes before the class began. Except now and then in math class, she never wrote things in her notes that had no meaning for her. She never let an unknown word or technical term slip by without definition or explanation. She became an accomplished listener; scraps of sentences that explained or clarified were extracted from even the most rambling and convoluted discourse. Her notes looked a mess. Around an outline or diagram there were things written at odd angles in margins, arrows connecting things or pointing to other notes, reminders to read certain pages or to look up some source. It wasn't pretty, but it worked because it all had to make sense as she wrote it. For her, review was really review; she didn't have to learn from scratch between classes.

Lectures take on a new meaning when they are seen as opportunities for learning—free tutoring from an expert. If a teacher is the best economist in the state, no serious student would skip her lectures. When you come to realize that education is your own doing and won't just happen, you will quickly begin taking advantage of the chance to rummage through the minds of experts. You'll think about the relevant questions at the moment when help is within reach, rather than putting them off to accumulate. Learning during the lecture reduces the time and effort a course would take if you had to do it all alone. Each lecture becomes a period of quality study time.

Making the Effort

I have compared the process of learning to the development of physical skills such as weightlifting or playing musical instruments. There are few physical or physiological similarities, to be sure, but both kinds of activity require similar habits of mind, and it is these that are of importance here. The idea of performance should underlie learning as surely as it does practicing the cello. The intent here is to suggest that neither weightlifting, nor practicing the cello, nor learning chemistry can be made easy. Interesting, satisfying, and rewarding, yes—but not effortless.

Attending class, in the proper sense, and especially the class of a more demanding teacher, will not be a relaxing period of easy listening. It can be rewarding, however, for two reasons. When your mind is tracking that of the teacher and her ideas are finding their way into your consciousness, you can hardly escape the enjoyment that comes from this "mature interplay of minds." When the necessary effort is made, both the facts of the discipline and the energy of the teaching will seep into your system. And then there is a second reward: a record of what has transpired in class, one that makes sense to you because you understood it as you wrote it. You will have notes that make clear to you what went on during that period.

Boredom

Obviously, I've portrayed the best of all possible worlds here. What about boredom? Many a student has entertained me with stories of courses of unrelenting and stupefying boredom. It is a serious problem with no simple answer. I would suggest that there might be three reasons for boredom in the classroom:

1. The subject might be boring, or at least perceived to be so.
2. The teacher's presentation might be boring.
3. It is possible that the student might be constituitively bored—that is, bored by nearly everything.

Starting at the bottom, consider the possibility that the cause of boredom lies with the student. Recall the box with $100,000 I described before. Suppose the instructions were accurate and reliable, but were given in French and your French is not all it might be. Being talked to in a language you don't know soon becomes boring. In this case, whether the speech remains boring would be entirely dependent on the listener. If enough effort were made to find out what was being discussed, interest would immediately perk up and the listener would scurry off to find a French dictionary. Without that initial effort, however, the talk is boring and you walk away from it (and from the $100,000). Being bored with the new and unfamiliar is not a bad sign. It just means you're becoming familiar with more things. Only after a sincere effort has been made to get a grasp on the unfamiliar may we look to the other sources of boredom.

Boring teachers fall into two categories: the apparently boring and the truly boring. The truly boring waste your time talking about their personal exploits and a lot of other things unrelated to the subject. If after several days you can't tell what the subject is from the lecture, you have a truly boring teacher. More often the boring teacher is only apparently so. Our exposure to television has planted the expectation of nearly continuous entertainment. No teacher can match the visual impact of television; those few who try seldom provide either good entertainment or good teaching. The problem stems from a confusion about the nature of the two things. Learning is language-oriented and linear. Ideas come in sequence and embedded in language. Following what's going on requires mental processing. Pictorial entertainment, on the other hand, washes over us and relieves the mind of work.

Done well, attending a lecture is more like reading a book than watching a show. A teacher pacing the floor and talking entirely off the cuff about the Russian revolution would not make good television. No sponsor would pay for it. But if that undramatic talk, delivered without a pitchman's flair, still informs and explains, that teacher cannot justifiably be said to be boring. When an instructor does not live up to our expectations, the problem could be the instructor, or it might lie in our expectations.

The subject matter is the easiest target when the problem is boredom—it can't defend itself, after all. In fact, we are on the thinnest ice when we attribute boredom to the subject itself. Rarely does a college curriculum offer a subject that, in and of itself, lacks interest for the human mind. When some subject that many people have devoted their lives to comes across as boring, it is likely that it has been unattractively packaged. By *packaging* I mean the telling of the story. The very life can be sucked out of a subject, for example, by bad writing. The publication of a book, by the way, is no assurance that it is a good book. This is particularly true of textbooks. Again—rarely, I hope—you may encounter a teacher who has an encyclopedic but superficial knowledge of a subject, and so never gets below the surface to whatever it is that entrances scholars in that field.

Very seldom, then, is boredom an insurmountable problem. First look to your own expectations. Are you looking to be entertained? Next, look to the content. What books were assigned? Are there better books? Have you read any? Are you listening to the content of the lecture and not just the style?

Remember, the idea is to learn, and learning is your own doing. Don't make your education totally dependent on teachers. You can learn a subject even when the teacher is not the best. If you do find yourself in the unusual situation where, in spite of your best efforts, neither the teacher, nor the text, nor the readings are able to inform, you should probably get out of that course. But be careful here, and be honest with yourself. It is remarkably easy to drop a course in college, and no one seems upset by your doing it. (Here, again, college personnel treat students as adults and assume every decision has been thoroughly examined.) Don't let dropping courses become a routine way of dealing with difficulties. You could develop a habit of avoiding what's challenging, a habit that would be hinted at by numerous "withdrawals" on your transcript.

Some Things to Remember

We might, at this point, use the ideas presented here for practice: Pretend the text is a lecture and you are to make notes. Can we, from this sea of words, construct a summary of what has been suggested to enable you to learn better during lectures? You might well generate a list such as the following:

- Go in prepared, either by reviewing or by reading ahead as needed.
- Listen to the words. Words have meaning.
- Internalize the meanings of words. Without thought, words are just sounds.
- Make notes on your own understanding of what you have heard. Paraphrase.
- Ask questions. Volunteer answers and comments.

Note two things about this list. First, nothing on the list is a simple behavior. Each entry suggests complicated activity that requires effort, particularly mental effort. As we have observed, learning is not the product of tricks or gimmicks. It is the process of engaging the mind with language, and the only way to do that is to do it. You can become very good at it in a relatively short time, but not by taking shortcuts.

Secondly, without the words that came before it, the list shown above is not very helpful. The point of a summary is to refresh the mind regarding all that has gone before. Items in a summary are of little use unless they suggest the details. A summary, in other words, is not a substitute for the material it summarizes. The words "Make notes on your own understanding of what you have heard," for example, do not by themselves suggest any new or different activity. They serve only as a reminder of the details in a long discussion on listening carefully, internalizing meanings, and paraphrasing.

If you are convinced by these ideas, you will see the lecture more as useful than as obligatory—a period of free tutoring and concentrated learning. Having a useful reason for attending, you will not fall into the habit of cutting classes. Most important, work between classes will be done with less difficulty and confusion. It is far easier to refresh your mind on something you have already worked through than to learn it from scratch, and with no expert on hand.

five

Reading

Student Voices

THE FINAL IS GOING TO COVER 230 PAGES! HOW
DO THEY EXPECT ANYONE TO DO ALL THAT IN
TWO DAYS?

—CELIA

 etween the last day of classes and the first day of final exams, many colleges have what is called the *reading day*. Whatever the inventors of that term had in mind, it certainly was not to suggest that all of a student's reading could be done in a day. The practice is mentioned here to illustrate that *to read* has more than one meaning. In fact, the actual meaning of *to read* evolves continually, from our earliest attempts to decode clumps of letters well into old age. We all read, but we are not all doing the same thing. That small fact has serious consequences for students who have been assigned something to read. Just as reading means something slightly different to each student, the teachers' understanding of reading might be much different from that of the students. Should that be the case, you might very well "read" and still not be doing what your teachers expect. A useful strategy would be to find out how your teachers read. Knowing that, you would be fairly sure that you are doing what they expect when you read.

Again, it is risky to say anything that is supposedly true of all teachers, but the one thing they all do is tell other people what they know. Some of what they know came from their own discoveries and from making original connections between things others have discovered, but a great deal of what they know came from reading. The fact that teachers instruct others and get much of their knowledge from reading causes them to read in a particular way. Most teachers read with the idea somewhere in their heads that they will, or they may, some day have to teach what they are learning. They read in what might be called "performance mode."

Clearly, recreational reading is not done with performance in mind, but any time teachers read in a content area they teach, or might teach some day, there is an intense need to get it right. The need to get it right focuses the mind. It is essential that they not miss the writer's intent or garble it, because some future lecture might depend on getting the message exactly right. When doing content reading, they would never read without making notes along the way. Few teachers trust their memories to retain the details, or the dates, or the author or title of the book or article.

Another thing teachers have learned is that they do not always need to read an entire book, or even a chapter, if they know in advance what they are looking for. Reading with the idea of instructing others, and reading in response to a need to find something in particular, are characteristics of a teacher's reading. Most teachers have this kind of reading in mind when they tell a student to read.

A new college student may be reading in a very different way. A great deal of student reading, for example, is from textbooks, and, except for mathematics and highly technical subjects, textbooks are generally not the best source if the intent is to learn. (If this sounds shocking, note that the eminent educator and philosopher Mortimer Adler thinks so little of textbooks that he advocates that they be banned from all schools.) Textbooks seldom captivate the mind; they tend to promote mechanical and shallow reading. Certainly anyone whose reading has been limited to textbooks could be forgiven for having developed a distaste for reading. When reading is distasteful it is done grudgingly—with a sense of duty.

Getting in Sync with Your Teachers

To make reading efficient, and perhaps to rediscover the joy of reading, try reading the way your teachers do. This means that you will pretend, while reading, that you will have to present this material to someone else. Every teacher will tell you that nothing focuses the mind so keenly as the need to prepare a lecture. By pretending that you are going to teach someone else, you provide yourself with the motivation to focus your mind and get a clear idea of what the writer has to say. In truth, this might not be entirely pretense. You may be called on during an exam to explain what some reading was about, and a good way to do that is to write the exam as if you were teaching someone else. When you are doing assigned reading, try pretending that *you* are going to present a lecture to your classmates on this topic. If you're good at pretending, you'll find that this technique will focus your mind wonderfully.

What to Read

We learn by reading, listening, writing, note making, speaking, painting, composing, and many other activities, but none of these things is effective if it is merely an activity done without engaging the mind. Two people might read the same pages, and one learns a great deal while the other is unchanged by the experience. Clearly, then, simply "doing the required readings" guarantees nothing. Even so, the first step toward effective reading is knowing what should be read and how to find it. Some teachers make it explicitly clear what they feel you should read by providing detailed reading assignments. However, it is those freewheeling teachers who hint and suggest who cause us difficulties. One teacher might have a syllabus that states, for each class period, the chapter of a textbook that should be read before the class meets. More advanced students find this a somewhat dreary approach, but at least there is no uncertainty about where to find the readings. Another teacher might provide a "reading list" of perhaps fifteen or twenty books and a number of magazine or journal articles, but never say anything more about the list. Those teachers who seem vague about the reading material will require more attention on your part.

Teachers who have not themselves been students for many years no longer depend on having someone tell them what pages or chapters of what books should be read. They have the habit of looking for information and opinion, and they search through a variety of sources to find what they need. The reading "suggestions" of such teachers might be subtle indeed. In the middle of a discussion of economic conditions a teacher might say, "These were the ideas of Keynes. So-and-so has several good chapters on Keynesian economics in his book." The experienced student will pick up on that hint immediately. In letters that can't be missed, he would write in his notes, "Keynesian econ. see So-and-so." Again, a biology teacher might say, "I assume you know the difference between mitosis and meiosis," and immediately proceed to something else. Never ignore such a broad hint. Should you have forgotten the details of mitosis and meiosis, or if you never really knew them, write the words in your notebook with exclamation points and a reminder, "Look up/learn."

Experienced students have learned, sometimes the hard way, that there are things they are responsible for and must learn, beyond those specific assignments given by a teacher. As you learn this subtle lesson, you will find that you are no longer reading pages or chapters, but topics and ideas. Studying Keynesian economics is a very different thing from "reading the chapter."

The difference here is not merely a matter of word choice. Reading a chapter because you are told to do so gives the whole process an air of obligation—of paying dues to keep in good standing. To be a learning process, reading must be approached with a bit of anticipation. Reading will never be profitable so long as it is perceived as an unpleasant duty. The one thing that will promote profitable reading is curiosity—a need to know. The sports enthusiast will always find a newspaper to check the scores. He certainly never has to ask anyone, "What page?" The phrase *Chapter 6,* without a suggestion of content, is certainly not going to stimulate anyone's curiosity. But *Keynes, mitosis, World War I, e. e. cummings,* and *the gas constant* are capable of arousing our curiosity. If mature, rational, and intelligent people such as your teachers find a topic interesting enough to read about, take a little time to find out why.

Much of what you read will be suggested by teachers. An assigned reading is clearly a strong suggestion. Less obvious suggestions you must learn to recognize. The name of an author, particularly if it appears on the reading list, is always a suggestion, as are topics that are mentioned as being important but not discussed in detail. After some time, serious students learn to sprinkle topics and authors' names around the edges of their notes and later spend some of their unscheduled time looking into these things. You can never tell when something important or interesting might turn up. This kind of reading embodies the major motivating factor that makes reading effective—the need to know.

Reading for Different Purposes

Reading for courses can be divided roughly into two major categories. Sometimes the reading—a book, for example—is approached "cold." This means you have no expectations about the contents except for what can be inferred from the title. This is the way we approach a book that is assigned without much explanation. The point of the assignment is very often to produce a review, or it may be to get a feel for some particular subject or to learn something about how the writer thinks. At other times, you take up a book because you know in advance that it contains some particular information you need. In such cases you may not intend to read the whole book, but to search through it until you find what you were looking for. You are approaching the book not with the intent of reviewing it, but as a resource for something you need to know.

The same book can be approached by two people in two quite different ways: One student might read Barbara Tuchman's *The March of Folly* to discover the common elements in some monumental historical blunders. Typically, that student would start at the beginning of the book and read it through. A second student might be looking for material on the causes of the American Revolution. That student might also pick up *The March of Folly,* but would likely skip the siege of Troy, the Renaissance popes, and Vietnam, and go directly to Chapter IV, "The British Lose America."

In either case, having the purpose of learning something is the necessary condition for useful reading. Reading with the intent and hope of learning something new guarantees that you will. Reading because it was assigned is the sad alternative.

Mechanics

Someone reading out of curiosity about a given topic really needs no help with mechanics. The need to know takes over the mind, which then does just what it must to satisfy that curiosity. An avid ice hockey fan finds out one way or another what a "hat trick" is. He would certainly not read the sports page every day and each time skip over the words "hat trick" because he didn't know what they meant. After looking for some specific information of interest to us, it would be strange indeed if we could not remember it once we had found it.

But we need to be realistic here. Some readings are going to be on subjects absolutely new to us. They might be on topics with which we have only the slightest familiarity. Even with good will and the best intentions, we may find the subject matter dry. Reading in these areas, particularly when it involves many pages or chapters of a book, is going to require some discipline and a mechanism to help us understand and keep track of large amounts of new material.

Reading a book or article for review, as we have seen, is somewhat different from using a book or article as a resource. A book is a resource when it has what you need to know embedded in a lot of other stuff that, for the moment at least, is of less interest to you. It is important to make this distinction because some less experienced readers will approach all reading as if it were done for review. Instead of searching for and finding what they need to know, they simply start at the beginning and try to remember everything that happens. Resource reading is more immediately satisfying because the difficult part is over when the need to know is experienced. You search, find, write it down, and the job is done. But when the task is to find out *everything* that a writer has to say, it's a good idea to approach the reading as if you were going to write a review.

A nonfiction book or article might be about history, biography, molecular genetics, bridge-building theory, literary criticism, economic theory, or any other topic someone got interested enough to write about. If the title is not a dead giveaway, you will be curious as to what the book is about. You can find this out by making some guesses based on chapter headings, or skipping around looking for key words. Since you're going to read most or all of the book in any event, I'm not sure what this accomplishes, but some people recommend it highly. The alternative is to trust that the writer is going to tell you what he is talking about, and just begin.

Reading of this kind is not very different from reading a story, and if the item is well written, it will indeed tell a story. What is quite different is that there will be many matters of fact, induction, argument, conjecture, theory, and deduction that you will need to know, understand, and remember. This means you must make notes on your reading.

There is no substitute for making notes; quite definitely, highlighting is not a substitute. People who love their highlighters will not want to give them up, but these gadgets really do not enhance learning. Marking words with a highlighter is satisfying because it gives the impression that one has captured something. The words are embalmed in pink, or yellow, or pale blue. But highlighting, like so many "easy" techniques, can be done without thought, and when it is, it accomplishes very little. (Besides, it's an act of vandalism if the book is not your own.) Everyone who makes notes consistently will eventually settle on a way of doing it that is useful and comfortable. If you don't already make useful notes on your reading, experiment with one of the methods described below.

Computer-Assisted Study

I f you know word processing, the computer becomes a very useful tool for developing notes on reading. It is seldom convenient to read while stopping frequently to type notes on a keyboard, however. Instead, try the following method to see if you are comfortable with it: Keep a pencil in hand while you read (not a pen or highlighter) and make notes lightly on the page next to sections that need to be thought about further. If the book is not yours, make notes on small Post-its and stick them to the page. Often it is sufficient to make code marks: Use a symbol or the letter q to indicate that you will want to quote this passage in your notes (no need to write it out yet); p might mean that you will want to paraphrase a paragraph or section; ? could mean that you need to reread that section again later; *See p. xx* might mean that you will want to draw connections later between two ideas. Each time you make a mark, note on a pad the page number where the mark occurs. After a few reading sessions, take the book and your pad to the computer and prepare your notes at the keyboard, using the page numbers on the pad to find your marks.

In the telling of it, this method may sound a bit awkward, but it has real advantages. Most people, particularly if they can touch-type, will write more at a keyboard than they would with a pencil. More ideas are recorded, and in greater detail. Also, this method requires a second reading of whatever it was you marked in the first place. Nothing aids the memory better than repetition. Furthermore, you will find that sometimes you cannot immediately remember why a passage was marked. That fact will prompt rereading and rethinking until the connection snaps back and you remember, like recognizing an old friend. Figuring it out twice is likewise a terrific aid to the memory. Finally, you have a neat, readable set of notes the instant you write them, and all the tricks of word processing are available. Notes can be supplemented as needed, re-arranged, and edited.

Without the Computer

If you are not yet computer-friendly, something similar can be done with pad and pencil. I still recommend that the initial reading be done with only small pencil marks and notations in the margin, or on Post-its, and the written notes be made at a later time. This suggestion may sound peculiar to you—why not do it all at once? There are two reasons. If the writing is well done it will flow along, with one idea leading logically into the next. Each time you stop, you interrupt the flow. The time taken to make a few light pencil marks will not distract you from the writer's train of thought. The second reason is more important: Writing notes at a later time requires going over the same material twice, even though you might spend much less time the second time. Working your way through someone else's thought patterns is a little like walking though dense underbrush. It's all new and foreign and sometimes you can't tell quite where you're going to end up or how you got where you are. Were you to make the same trip a day later, things would be quite different. Your first trip left marks. You are following something like a path: trees and rocks that were obstacles before become landmarks. A third trip would be a breeze. This is not a totally fanciful analogy for the effect of new ideas on the brain. An idea moving through the thinking part of the brain leaves a track. A second trip follows the first track and reinforces it.

Language

What would a very learned person say was of the essence in effective schooling? Wise people have indeed thought about this, and have reached something of a consensus: An educated person knows how to listen to, read, write about, and discuss significant ideas. To be sure, there are many hidden assumptions and definitions lurking in this description. *Significant,* for example, would not likely include the details of the private lives of sit-com stars. To *discuss* means more than to express an opinion, and *listening* means more than hearing. The point is that each of these activities hinges on the ability to find the meaning behind words. Listening is just hearing if the words make no mental impact. Reading is little more than "looking at" unless the words are more than just familiar, but have clear and unambiguous meanings.

Without language, learning is nothing more than training: what we do to animals to get them to do tricks.

Words, Words, Words

Words, then, are of the essence. A very young child picks up a ball one day and says "Ball." Her parents go bonkers, and she quickly learns that she can get their undivided attention by pointing to things and making the right sounds. She is learning that words stand for things. Later she will discover that marks (writing) stand for words, and she will pester her parents by asking repeatedly, "What's that say?" A child's curiosity about language is the best proof that the human mind is pleased by learning.

The vast majority of the things we learn—everything except original discoveries—come from the magical transmission of thoughts from one head to another. The means of doing this is mankind's greatest invention, and its name is language. Reading, then, is our attempt to discover what is in the mind of another. It is considerably more complex than seeing symbols and hearing their equivalent sounds in our heads. Unless an idea emerges, nothing has been accomplished.

The longer our schooling goes on, the more subtle and complex are the things we will be expected to learn. The expression of subtle and complex ideas requires subtle and complex words. The metaphysics of consciousness, for example, cannot be simply dismissed as "wicked awesome," even though it is that. This and many another complex topic will require a large and active vocabulary if reading is to do what it was invented to do: capture another's ideas.

The Paraphrase

Reading, then, is turning out to be something of a challenge. How does anyone know whether they're doing it properly? I hinted at this problem when I talked about reading with the intent of producing a review, or reading with the idea of performance—presenting the writer's ideas to someone else. The idea there is that a review might serve as a test for a correct reading. However, adding even these aspects to reading is still not quite enough, because it is possible, in fact, to write an acceptable review of a book or article without understanding the original. By condensing the writing, picking topic sentences, and changing a few words, it is possible to reduce a book to five or ten pages. The process does indeed require a certain skill and some practice, but it is possible to produce a review in this way without learning anything of substance. It's a sterile exercise that thwarts the purpose of reading.

Better than a review, and almost guaranteed both to cause learning and to demonstrate it, is the paraphrase—at least the paraphrase as defined here. The paraphrase is probably the most intellectually demanding activity, after original discovery, that can be expected of a person. First we need to clear the mind of misconceptions—to weed out those things a paraphrase is *not*. The paraphrase is not just a review, nor a summary, abstract, synopsis, or condensation. To produce a high-quality example of any of these, a paraphrase would likely be required first, but it is still essentially different and separable. Let's look at what the mind goes though in the process of paraphrasing:

1. Reading and listening both start with someone else's words. These words must be internalized by you, the reader or listener. This means that you are consciously aware of all the words and the order in which they come. Awareness requires that you be alert and have your attention focused. The words must "register" in your head.

2. Unlike a computer, your brain does not store all the words in their exact sequence, at least not for long. Almost instantaneously it abstracts the meaning of key words and analyzes the grammatical arrangement to get a picture. You cannot get a picture if some of the key words are unknown to you and therefore make no contribution. Consider the following fragment: "He every day becomes more adroit and less industrious. . . ." If the word *adroit* happens not to be in your vocabulary, an accurate picture cannot emerge. But your mind does form the best picture it can. You are aware of some person who seems to be doing something day after day, but with decreasing energy and enthusiasm. If you know the word *adroit,* or look it up, then you see that this person is also becoming more skillful day after day. Symbols (words) have produced a mental image.

3. Once the words make sense and an image emerges, you must discover the writer/speaker's intent. What or whom is being talked about? Why are these particular words used and arranged in just that way? This is the most demanding aspect of listening or reading. The real intent of discursive speech or writing is to virtually reconstruct the ideas and thought of the writer/speaker in the head of the reader/listener. The danger here is being satisfied with your own perceived or imagined picture instead of first finding out what the writer/speaker wanted you to think. In the example given above, you might wonder what conditions would cause skill to increase while enthusiasm decreased. The answer is there somewhere in the words— that was the writer/speaker's intent. But unless that intent can be discovered, the primary goal of language has been missed.

4. Only now are you ready to make notes—to paraphrase. When you know the writer/speaker's thoughts and intentions, you must formulate language from your own vocabulary, using your own grammatical constructions, to express anew those same thoughts. The writer/speaker's thoughts (even if you happen not to agree with them) are in one sense your thoughts, because they are now in your head. You now use new language to transmit these thoughts to paper.

The essential aspect of the paraphrase lies in the words "formulate language from your own vocabulary, using your own grammatical constructions." Students encountering these ideas for the first time wonder, understandably, why using their own vocabulary and constructions is so important. Is there something wrong with the original? The quality of language in the original is not the issue. Some paraphrases use simpler language than the original, others more complex; some are an improvement on the original and some are not. The importance of the paraphrase is that it forces ideas through the thinking part of the brain. Using the original language might well be a matter of merely copying the unknown. When language you generate on your own turns out to mean the same as the original, you prove to all that you understand.

If you do capture and internalize words, extract meaning, reconstruct the original intent, and formulate new language to express the same ideas, an unbelievable number of synapses will have fired in your brain. Had your head been scanned during the process, hot spots would show up where energy was being used. The process is intrinsically strenuous; it cannot be made easy. It is nevertheless enjoyable and very satisfying. It's learning in the best sense of the word.

Reading Versus Listening

In certain subjects, students, if they happen to be blessed with a good lecturer, will try, sometimes with considerable success, to get by with listening and skip the reading. Certainly students who score well on exams without reading anything but their class notes have learned the fine art of listening and are to be commended for it. It remains true, however, that listening, for all its merits, is not a substitute for reading.

It is tempting to believe that listening is an easier way to learn than reading. Certainly listening itself is easier than reading. That is because the listener can sit passively and let it happen. But learning, as we have discovered, is neither easy nor passive. In fact, learning by listening alone is more difficult than learning through reading. There are several reasons. You cannot ask a speaker to shut down for a spell while you ponder what was just said. You are not likely to ask him to repeat the last three sentences. These things can be done, however, when you read. Those few exceptional students who get by in demanding courses by means of careful listening and note making alone, would improve their learning enormously by adding reading and paraphrasing to their arsenal.

Scholars who research the learning process itself would also add that students who get by without reading are preparing themselves poorly for the future. A productive and satisfying life will require ongoing learning long after college is over. Reading is one of those habits of the mind that empowers us and makes possible lifelong learning. The earlier habits are acquired, the more readily they become ingrained. If you don't already have the reading habit, college may represent the last best opportunity.

six

Writing

Student Voices

AT THE END OF A COURSE YOU SHOULD BE ABLE TO
WRITE A ONE-PAGE PAPER THAT WOULD TELL SOMEONE
WHAT YOU'VE LEARNED. IF YOU CAN'T DO IT, YOU'VE
WASTED YOUR TIME.

—CHRIS

 most reliable indicator of an educated person is the ability to produce clear, informative writing. It is also true, however, that writing clearly and informatively is a most powerful way to learn. We appear to have another chicken-egg problem. It seems you need to be well educated to write, but you need to write to become educated. How do you get started?

The paradox arises from the assumption that you need to have one thing done before you start the other. The paradox disappears when we discover that understanding and writing both improve in small increments and they reinforce one another. Neither needs to be completed before the other. Learning and writing operate on one another in a way scientists call "positive feedback." Imagine someone had tinkered with your car, fixing it so that the speedometer reading was connected to the gas pedal. As the needle moved higher on the speedometer, more gas would be fed to the engine. The smallest forward motion of the car would start the speedometer upward, increasing the flow of gas. More gas would mean faster motion, which in turn would mean more gas and still greater speed. Such positive feedback gives rise to what is called a "runaway" condition. In this somewhat frightening example, it would mean constantly increasing and uncontrollable speed until the limit of the engine was reached.

Runaway Learning

If writing and learning are indeed linked in a positive feedback loop, the results could be remarkable: Just getting the process started would cause "runaway learning." A little writing causes a little learning, a little learning makes for better writing, and the learning/writing process has been set in motion. Like all analogies, this one has some sizable holes, but it offers hope because progress is possible regardless of your starting level. And even with its holes, I doubt that many teachers would argue with the general truth and usefulness of the theory.

One major problem with the theory is the vagueness of the word *write*. This is the reason I emphasized the words *clear* and *informative* above. Virtually all college students can write, sometimes quite expressively and imaginatively. Too often, however, college instructors in history, psychology, business, science, and other disciplines find student writing to be—in polite terms—inadequate. It is common for students to earn acceptable marks on freshman English papers, only to find their written work in other disciplines severely criticized. Teachers in these other disciplines often find that student writing is unclear, lacks coherence, or misses the point. It is worth our time to try to get to the cause of this problem.

Two Purposes for Writing

Writing has two important functions. The well-understood purpose can be called *evaluative*. This means that writing in some format is used to demonstrate knowledge, understanding, or, at the very least, that some work has been done. Teachers use student writing to determine how well the student is learning—that is, to evaluate student progress. Progress is indicated by grades and by something we call "credit."

Evaluative Writing

For a few teachers, and nearly all new college students, evaluation is the only point of writing. Given a suggestion or an assignment that involves writing, our first impulse is to ask, "Do we have to hand this in?" The belief that all academic writing is evaluative, to be credited to one's account, interferes with the more important goal of writing—to learn something about the topic. These two purposes of writing can be considered separately.

Writing to Learn

Learning is the less familiar purpose of writing. Many students mistakenly believe that writing can be done only after the learning is done. It appears at first that they have logic on their side. How can you write about something unless you know it? It can be done; in fact, it's done every day in college and is a most effective way to learn, but to do it you must see writing as having purposes other than evaluation.

Let's think of writing as simply putting words on paper. When you think "writing," you should include, for example, making notes—something that should be occupying a good deal of your time. You make notes to record and make sense of a lecture period or a reading assignment. This kind of writing is seldom handed in, but it can be and should be an occasion of learning. It can, on the other hand, be a mindless mechanical activity if there is no intent to learn or if the relationship between writing and learning is not appreciated.

As noted before, machines such as tape recorders, camcorders, and photocopiers are far more reliable transcription machines than a human with a pencil. Were learning just a matter of storing and retrieving, we could leave it all to machines. Serious learning does something to the mind, however. Learning affects the brain in a way that storing does not affect a computer. If you instruct a computer to delete the "elephant" file, it will do so and you will never again get a hint from the computer that it has ever before encountered elephants. Tell a human not to think about elephants for two minutes and they find that command absolutely impossible to carry out. The concept *elephant*, having entered the brain, has altered it permanently—the *idea* of *elephant* cannot be erased, short of physical violence.

We don't know in any detail how the brain does this. But the fact is certain sounds stimulate some part of the brain and we are powerless to block the picture or concept they summon up. This kind of brain activity makes language extraordinarily potent. The word *elephant* pulls up a picture; a picture or drawing of the animal, in turn, brings up the word. It's really all quite remarkable, and something we can hardly do anything about. Try to not think about elephants!

To appreciate the way your mind works, imagine that someone asks you to talk for two minutes about elephants. You would not say, "I'm sorry, I don't know anything about elephants." That would clearly be an exaggeration. Neither you nor anyone else knows everything about elephants, but nearly everyone knows something. It is true that you have probably not memorized a lot of data on elephants, such as average height, weight, life span, or the number living in Africa. You do have an image, however. What you would have to do is put together, from scratch, word groups (sentences) that describe what your mind is visualizing and remembering. You would be able to do this because, little by little, over the years, you have indeed learned something about elephants. Not set pieces to be recited, but bits and scraps of things—stuff that can be pushed and prodded into sentences.

Learning in college needs to be a lot like your learning about elephants. Something needs to be lodged in the brain so that it will pop up on demand, in sufficient detail that you can formulate language to describe accurately what the brain has recalled. Suppose now that you are asked to talk for two minutes about peroxisomes. Unless you are well versed in biology, you will be at a loss for words—literally. There are no words because there is no picture. The brain has not been permanently modified by previous encounters with *peroxisomes;* the word is just a sound and it conjures up no picture.

Learning

Writing is a good way to burn ideas into the brain. To do so, however, it must be the kind of writing that actually activates the thinking part of the mind. Mechanically transcribing words from one page to another does not require that the words be thought about. It can be done quite accurately while the mind is actively engaged elsewhere. That kind of writing does nothing permanent to the brain and does not cause learning. Writing causes learning when the words are firmly associated with thoughts or ideas. The reason you know something about elephants is that the first time you saw one, you asked, "What's that?" The *idea* of *elephant* is so overwhelmingly impressive that it burns itself forever into the brain. All you need after that is words. *Peroxisome,* on the other hand, if it is not an idea or concept in your mind, will not be learned just because the word is stored in your short-term memory. So long as it remains only a word, it is not learned. You will be like the computer; if the word is lost, there is nothing left.

So if mere transcription will not cause learning, what kind of writing will do it? Actually, if you have read Chapter 5, "Reading," you already know. It's paraphrasing. Paraphrasing is not mechanical transcription. It consists of generating language to transmit ideas or concepts that are more or less well understood. "More or less" is a key phrase. The first attempt to write on paper what you think you understand can be frustrating. The "I know it but I can't say it" problem returns. Such frustration is a good sign. It makes you keenly aware that you need to learn. If you can't say it, why not? There are only two good reasons:

1. You forgot.
2. The original words (someone else's) did not have real meaning for you.

The second reason is the important one. Serious writing involves subtlety, and that means having a somewhat sophisticated vocabulary. If a writer says that something is terrific or that it stinks, you know how the writer feels about it, but you're still not informed about the thing itself. Accurate descriptions involve complex words. What would it mean, for example, if something were said to be enervating, palpable, ineluctable, mendacious, scintillating, coruscating, palatable, excoriating, or rapacious? There is a lot more to knowing a thing than just knowing that it is good or bad, or that somebody liked it or didn't. Serious learning often involves making subtle distinctions, and these distinctions can be expressed only through language. There is no substitute for knowing words and using them appropriately.

Words

No one is born with a vocabulary. All words are learned. Our vocabulary swells as soon as we learn to read because writing tends to condense the language. That is, writing compresses ideas into a smaller number of words, but these words, to do more work, are more complex. Children reading on their own will repeatedly ask "What's this word mean?" when they come upon words they don't use in speech. If reading stops being satisfying (from being forced to read bad writing, perhaps), we no longer care what it means. Getting to the end becomes the goal. We start skipping over words we don't recognize. We have lost our curiosity. Skipping unfamiliar words is a deadly habit. It must be broken if you intend to learn.

Paraphrasing

You will learn through writing if that writing involves, to some degree, the paraphrase. Let's see how language and vocabulary relate to the paraphrase. A very learned person might paraphrase several pages of a book in a paragraph that looks, to the less learned, more complicated and less comprehensible than the original. What that reader has done is to put the original ideas into words familiar to her, but, having a large vocabulary, she has produced a paraphrase more dense and complex than the original. This is perfectly consistent with the intent of the paraphrase. It is not intended to simplify. A paraphrase forces the mind to understand so thoroughly that the content of the original can be accurately restated in the vocabulary of the writer's choice. Whether the words used are simpler than those in the original or more complex is not the issue.

Either way, if you are writing to learn, the paraphrase can have only words that mean something to you. Writing words that do not have meaning for you makes you a slow and inefficient copying machine. Learning is not taking place. Furthermore, big or technical words do not explain; they are merely shortcuts for people who already know their meaning. Writing a paraphrase is possible only when the intent of the original is known. Knowing intent demands knowing, or learning, the meaning of all the words.

The question remains, why is it necessary to actually write one's understanding of someone else's language? Why isn't it enough to do it all mentally? Simply put, it's because we're very good at conning ourselves. Now and then you find a person who is truly a "quick study"—someone who can quickly capture and comprehend a complex problem or issue. Such people are actually fairly rare. The rest of us tell ourselves that we can understand everything we read, but when put to the test, we find ourselves saying, "I know it but I can't say it." Writing, therefore, if it is a paraphrase and not merely a transcription, is an immediate test. You find out instantly whether or not you understand what you have read or heard. The inability to write a paraphrase is a clear indicator that the original was not really understood. You are forced to go again to the original and think some more, learn the vocabulary, discover the intent—in short, to learn.

Writing produces learning, then, but in an indirect way—by forcing understanding of the spoken or written word. Writing provides an instant test of understanding. What cannot be paraphrased still needs to be learned. Writing of this kind, then, is a learning technique. As such, it can be used in a variety of situations. Suppose, for example, you have a course in which the teacher presents material so rapidly, and in such a condensed way, that you hardly have time to reflect on what you are writing. Your study time for such a course might be spent almost entirely in paraphrasing your own class notes. Note that I did not say *copying* your class notes. Some students copy their own notes, but the only intent seems to be to improve the penmanship. Copying does not clarify or explain. Paraphrasing class notes with a text or other source at hand (and a dictionary) is one of the most profitable ways to spend some of your unscheduled time (see Chapter 7, "Between Classes").

Paraphrasing is useful for another reason. Students often complain that a book or other reading assignment is "difficult." They read it, but it simply makes no sense. On occasion such reading material may indeed be conceptually challenging. On the other hand, it might be a case of bad writing. Experts in clear writing style take delight in quoting a passage of convoluted and inflated prose, and then paraphrasing it in clear language. The following is an example from Joseph Williams's book, *Style:*

> *The adolescents who had effectuated forcible entry into the domicile were apprehended.*

Once Williams had extracted meaning from this awful clutter of words, he paraphrased it as follows:

> *We caught the kids who broke into the house.*

The original was not really difficult in the sense of conceptually challenging; it was a simple idea, very badly stated. You should not assume that books or articles, simply because they appear in print, are always well written. Writing to learn, in some instances, will involve no more than stripping the original source of pompous, inflated language. Get to the meaning. Expressing ideas is the principal purpose of language. The language might be straightforward and simple or convoluted and complex, but there is always (or almost always) some idea embedded there. Capture the idea in your own language and you have learned something. You will also be able to tell someone else what you know.

Evaluative Writing

This brings us to the second purpose of academic writing. Writing to be submitted is nearly always evaluative, meaning that it is used to judge progress. Writing that is used to evaluate student progress is graded, and grades are important.

This may be the first time I have said anything substantial about grades. Grades are important because they are what might be called signifiers. They signify accomplishment. Strangely enough, grades are important only because there are some low ones. Consider an imaginary high school where any student who attended one half of the class sessions for a course would receive an A for that course. What would it signify if you had a straight-A average from that school? Or imagine a world where college football games were arranged by referees so that every game ended in a tie and each team was declared the winner. What would be the significance of an undefeated season?

These examples demonstrate that grades and rankings have significance only when they honestly reflect accomplishment. There is something hollow about a high grade that you can't be proud of. Most people who have already been through this will tell you: Learn well and the grades will take care of themselves.

Students complain about grades, but complain again if there aren't any. The reason is straightforward: Everyone wants to know whether they are doing well. "Am I making progress?" If it is your writing that is to be graded or ranked, you want that writing to accurately reflect what you know, and that means you must write well.

Your most helpful teachers will get you started by supplying details and hints about a writing assignment:

1. What is the topic?
2. What is the intent?
3. Who are you writing for?
4. What are the expected format and scope?
5. What is the due date?
6. Is the first submitted version the one that will be graded?

Let's assume such a detailed assignment has been given. Why are these details important? First, the *topic*. Letting you choose your own topic is not necessarily a good thing. The teacher might find the topic you chose to write about to be trivial, but you wouldn't know that until it was too late. When everyone writes on the same topic, you all start on a level playing field.

The *intent* of an assignment must be understood. Is it a broad review of a very big topic or a narrow review of a smaller topic? Perhaps it isn't a review at all. Maybe you are expected to compare different points of view on the topic. Or you may be asked to record your personal reaction to a topic or to what has been written about a topic. Very often the intent is to explain something. In all of these cases, content-based assignments will require reading. There aren't many people in the world who are prepared to write a factual essay entirely from memory. So, again, the paraphrase will play an important role in your writing.

Your Audience

The question of *who is being addressed* in your writing may seem strange, but writing with some actual or imagined person in mind is a great help. Whoever is being addressed is sometimes referred to as your *audience,* and I will use that term here. The audience is the person or group that you have in mind as your write. Upon being asked to write about *Henry V,* the first question you should ask is, "Who wants to know?" Most students assume the teacher is the audience. Some other books on college learning reinforce this idea and urge students to remember that the person they are writing for is the teacher—an audience of one. In general, this is not good advice. I would write for the teacher as audience only if the teacher expressly stated that I was to do so. Why is writing for the teacher not a good idea? It's because teachers are always assumed to be the final authority, and students tend to think it unnecessary to tell teachers what they already know. If you write for the teacher, you'll tend to use specialized words without defining them, or leave out background and detail because you consider them unnecessary. So ask about audience. Later I'll suggest a useful imaginary audience if you're left on your own.

Scope and format are important, but these words may not mean exactly what you think. Scope is not the same as length, for example, and there is more to format than footnotes and references. A preoccupation with the number of pages to be written or the number of sources to be cited springs from a misunderstanding of the intent of the writing. Being overly concerned with these matters suggests that the writing is going to be done merely to please the teacher. The real purpose of the writing, remember, is to learn something and then to inform your audience of what you have learned. Approximate length is important, of course—you will approach an assignment of two or three pages very differently from one of twenty to thirty pages. But exact length is determined by the topic and the amount of detail your audience wants. The imaginary reader may want to read a newspaper-style article or the equivalent of a chapter in a book. Knowing what your audience wants to read determines how you write, and how much.

Not all teachers suggest an audience when assigning writing. If nothing at all is said about who you should have in mind while writing, create an imaginary person who wishes to learn about the assigned topic. One useful idea is to imagine a student, someone you don't know, who is home sick and is paying you to explain the assigned subject to him or her. If you have a vivid imagination, you might convince yourself that your imaginary student comes from a very wealthy family and there might be a bonus if the student does well as a result of your written tutoring.

Find out when the writing is due and mark your calendar. Finally, be sure to find out whether your first submitted draft is the one that will be graded. Sometimes a teacher will read a draft and make comments, then allow revisions before grading the final version. This is of tremendous benefit to the student, but not many teachers do it. If the draft you submit is the final one, the paper that will be graded, you will need to start early to allow time for final editing and rewriting.

Getting Started

We are concerned here with writing that is to be evaluated—given a grade or credit. Even so, the primary purpose is still to learn something. All assignments, including writing, are to be used to learn, not merely endured. So what do you do first if you are assigned to write a paper on, say, World War II? I think I would begin writing something immediately, before doing any reading. Sounds backwards. But I would do this to show myself what I didn't know about World War II. I would write sentences that pretended to describe the war and leave blanks for the facts I did *not* know. Something like this: "WWII occurred between the years _____ and _____. The fighting took place primarily in _____ and _____. The following countries were involved: _____. The precipitating events were _____. The leaders of the countries involved at the time were _____." I would continue in this way until all the aspects of war that I could think of had been included in these incomplete sentences.

The point of this kind of writing is that it forces you to formulate most of the questions anyone would ask if they wanted to know about a war. It also points out clearly some of the things you need to learn to write your paper. When you have written as many of these incomplete statements as you can think of, you're ready to do the reading.

So with several books on World War II on hand, you begin to learn what you don't know about the war. Collect the books, your incomplete statements, pencils, and lots of paper. As a general rule, how much you need to learn will depend on the length of the writing you need to do. You would probably not need to read every word of a 2,000-page text in order to write a two-page paper. Even so, that 2,000-page book might be very valuable should it be a good source of facts to fill in your incomplete statements. (You may, some day, want to read all of that big book if this little paper triggers an interest in World War II.)

As you read, you will be looking first for facts to fill in your incomplete statements. The idea here is to erase the "reading as punishment" attitude that some students bring to college. Writing sentences with blanks gives you a reason to read. So long as you are reading to find out things you need to know, it can't be boring. Your attention will not shut off after 15 minutes (as has sometimes been suggested) if you are continuing to discover things you need to know.

If you're reading to get answers, you'll read with attention, so you'll discover many facts that you hadn't even thought about when you wrote your incomplete statements. If these are interesting and will contribute to your audience's understanding, add them to your notes. A good technique for writing an assignment is to pretend you're writing a section for a textbook and you want the reader to have a good understanding of the topic. Constantly remind yourself that you're teaching your audience.

We need to reflect here on two aspects of writing in content areas, meaning disciplines other than English courses in writing. In such writing there are matters of fact and matters of opinion. What you write must not contain errors of fact. You cannot use your opinion when you give the date and place a treaty was signed. In content writing it is quite possible to be in error, so always get your facts straight.

Second, judgments that you do make, such as the significance of an event, a person's motivation, or contingent events (what might have happened had things been different) should be based on evidence. It is not true that any opinion is as good as any other. Your best and most interesting writing will come when you have developed the ability to make logical and sensible judgments based on factual evidence.

What you produce to begin, then, will be pages of notes on the topic of the assignment. Note, however, that the notes you create were made in response to things you had decided in advance that you needed to know, or in connection with items you came across while looking for these "need-to-know" answers. The other method—open to page one, line one, and read in the hope that something interesting will turn up—is quite dreary by comparison. If you try to read with no clue as to what you're looking for, your attention will indeed drift, probably in less than 15 minutes.

Once you have sorted out your notes and have, both in your head and on paper, a set of facts that carry the message you intend to deliver, you have nearly completed the main purpose of writing: to learn about the topic. Now the evaluative part needs to be addressed—you'd like a grade that reflects what you've learned. This part of the writing may be every bit as difficult as the first part.

Good writing, even if the topic is engineering or chemistry, has the elements of storytelling. This does not mean that it is fictional or that it must be humorous or entertaining. It only means that writing should let the reader know who is doing what to whom, and for what reason—or what is happening to what and with what effect, and why is it happening. In most cases, you would do well to start your writing with the understanding that you are going to tell someone a true story.

The one thing writing must not be is dull. But please note well, the opposite of *dull* is not *silly*. Don't start a paper, "O.K., dude, listen up," or "Once upon a time there were two electrons." Content writing is informative, interesting, and serious; it's not the place to be cute.

Here are some hints on avoiding one particular fault that readers (and teachers) find most objectionable: "Lacks coherence" is a very common comment on student papers. What it means is that the paper made no sense to the reader. Coherence means a kind of hanging together. When you dump a jigsaw puzzle out of its box, the pieces lack coherence, both physically and pictorially. Certainly all the elements of a sensible picture are contained in the pieces, but only their correct ordering and positioning allow the picture to emerge. If your writing is said to lack coherence, that doesn't mean that it doesn't have the facts, or that it is untrue, or that things have been left out; it means that you haven't told a story. All the elements of a picture are there, but for some reason there is still no picture.

I have two suggestions to help with the coherence problem. (Remember, I'm assuming you have enough correct information in the form of notes to write a coherent paper—you couldn't do the jigsaw puzzle if half the pieces were missing.) First, stories are a little like complete sentences: they have a beginning, a middle, and an end. So divide a page into three parts and decide what goes into each part. The beginning should lead the reader somewhat gently into the topic. It should define specialized language and provide any background information the reader will need in order to understand what is to follow. You are preparing the ground. The middle has all the new and explanatory stuff; the end sets the reader down—again, gently.

That's the easy part (like turning all the jigsaw pieces picture-side up and sorting them by color). Now the sentence-by-sentence writing must begin. It is here that the coherence problem reappears, more gruesome than before. Some student papers appear to be little more than a series of statements in random sequence. A serious coherence problem is the lack of continuity between sequential sentences. That's teacher-talk for "This sentence has no relationship with the one just before it." Lack of continuity can ruin your best attempts, but there is a relatively simple cure if you first understand the cause.

Inexperienced writers often work hard to get a particular idea into words; more experienced writers do the same. Unfortunately, too many inexperienced writers consider every sentence to be "history" once the period is in place. Many freshmen have admitted to me that they never read what they have written. The words trickle out a few at a time until the period arrives, and they seldom look back at the whole thing. They proceed instead with a new sentence, actually unaware of what the previous one said or even whether it made sense or not. So here is an important rule: Never start a new sentence until you have read the one you just finished. Sounds simple, but if you do it with the honest intent of telling a smooth and seamless story, you will write only sentences that follow logically from the ones that precede them. Writing only sentences that are linked or related to the preceding ones will create continuity and each paragraph will have coherence.

If you have not written this way before, it will help to go off somewhere and read out loud what you have written. Hear the words and ask yourself, "Would this make sense if it were someone else's writing?" Still better, have someone else read your writing to you. It can be quite educational to hear someone else reading your own words back to you. You may find yourself saying "That's not what I meant!" The lesson is clear: If it's not what you mean, don't write it.

One obvious outcome of this reading and rereading of your own writing is that the finished product is almost never the first thing that goes down on paper. *Revise and rewrite* is the name of the game. When you hit a truly clunky sentence, don't try to fix it. Ask yourself, instead, "What was I trying to say?" Then cross out the clunker and start over. Paper is the cheapest and most useful learning tool at your disposal. Don't be afraid to use it.

One more tip. Inexperienced writers love pronouns—those little all-purpose words: *it, this, these,* and *they.* The writer usually has something in mind that it stands for, but the reader doesn't know what that is if the writer has not made it absolutely clear. I really believe that student writing would improve by about 50 percent if students all made a firm promise that they would never again start a sentence with *It, This, These, Those, They,* or *That.* Why is this generally bad practice? The reason is that the previous sentence frequently has two, three, or more different things of importance. When the next sentence starts with *This,* the reader is very unsure of what *This* refers to. Obviously there are times when sentences may be started with these words, and that is when there is only one thing the pronoun could possibly refer to. So check your sentences that start with pronouns. If there is the slightest possibility that the reader won't know what *this* stands for, then replace *this* with the real thing.

The Mechanics

If you haven't already done so, learn to use a word processor. Some of my earlier comments might lead you to believe that I do not hold computers in very high regard. In fact, I like computers, but not when they are used simply as electronic books that supply instant answers, or when they are used to solve problems that the user doesn't even understand. Whenever computers reduce mental activity, or substitute for it, they are counterproductive. At their best, computers leave the mental stuff for the user and provide help by doing the tedious, mindless things. It is just here that they can help improve writing, and therefore learning. There are programs that teach touch-typing if you have never used a keyboard. (Many people get by with the two-finger method, but there is some advantage, and enormous satisfaction, in looking at the computer screen while you type and watching your ideas becoming words.) But the great boon for writing are the several excellent word processing programs.

Word processing allows unlimited rearranging and deleting, inserting and moving of letters, words, sentences, and paragraphs. You can try alternative sentences while saving the old ones for comparison. You can write two or more versions of a paragraph, or the whole paper, and combine parts of each to make a third (and save all three). Word processors are fun to use, and they encourage revision and rewriting, which almost always improve the final product. They also check spelling and (I guarantee this) actually improve your own spelling by reminding you patiently and repeatedly every time you misspell a word. Finally, they produce a typed copy for your audience.

A Word About Style

Style can be thought of as the impression your writing leaves with the reader, above and beyond the direct meaning embedded in the words. A reader might find your writing *choppy, simplistic, pompous, windy, disjointed, friendly, direct, compact, dense, clear, vague, opaque, shallow, stiff, stilted, free and easy, engaging, elegant,* or any of a host of other adjectives. You don't want your writing to sound pompous or choppy or disjointed. Is there some way to make it clear, engaging, and elegant? Well, there are books on the subject and you can get them from the library, but I suspect most writers of clear, engaging, and elegant prose developed their talent not from reading style books, but by reading clear, engaging, and elegant writing. In short, attractive writing is easy to identify and very difficult to describe.

If you have a "tin ear" for sentences, you can improve your style by reading good writers. I suggest Lewis Thomas's *Lives of a Cell* and *The Medusa and the Snail* to start.

Writing Is Hard Work

Our recurring theme in these pages is that learning cannot be made easy, in the sense that it can be done effortlessly or with the mind disengaged. Writing is an important element of learning, and writing well will require effort. However, being able to state, in clear and precise language, what you have come to understand brings great satisfaction. You will say some day that it was worth the effort.

All writing takes time and requires effort, even if it is not well done or if nothing is learned in the process. But writing without learning is boring as well as difficult, and provides no satisfaction. Writing provides another example of our central theme: Learning requires doing the difficult, but mere activities do not guarantee learning *just because* they are difficult. Learning comes from doing the right things. It seems a waste to spend time and energy writing and not to learn while doing it. Writing is hard work either way; why not engage the mind and learn as you go?

seven

Between Classes

Student Voices

THIS WOMAN IS RUINING MY LIFE. SHE THINKS I HAVE
NOTHING TO DO BUT READ PSYCHOLOGY. DON'T
TEACHERS UNDERSTAND WE HAVE OTHER CLASSES?
I WORK—I JUST DON'T HAVE THE TIME.

—SARAH

As we have seen, you can learn a great deal from classes or lectures, provided you listen with attention, make useful notes, and make the new words part of your working vocabulary. But the hours between classes likewise present learning opportunities. Actually you spend only about 15 hours a week in class. If you live at home, or were lucky enough to find a quiet dorm, you'll sleep about 60 hours a week. Maybe you have a part-time job that takes 20 hours each week. Give yourself 12 hours a week for eating and 6 more for showering and brushing teeth, shaving or makeup. Add 6 hours for getting from here to there and shopping, and 9 hours for jogging, basketball, tennis, or whatever. That should about fill up the week, right? Not quite; there are still 40 hours left in your week—the same amount of time most people spend at their full-time jobs! True, I have not considered sun time, TV time, and hanging-out time; that will come later. For now, the point is to break the habit of saying "I don't have time."

Priorities

We have stumbled onto a serious problem here. Even those who should know better will still say "I don't have time." But obviously, we all get 168 hours a week; no one has any more or any less time than anyone else. What we have are different priorities. What we do during our 168 hours demonstrates absolutely what our priorities are. Whatever is personally and privately important to us will always get done. Someone who spends 40 hours each week hanging out or couching in front of the TV is simply demonstrating what's important to him. People who are into bodybuilding will get in their gym time no matter what. Some "soap" addicts will drop any class that runs into their TV time, even if it means having to take an overload later. You will occupy your 40 unscheduled hours in a way that satisfies you, doing things that are interesting, distracting, pleasurable, or just comfortable through habit, but definitely important to you. Our goal here is to make learning important; then it is guaranteed to get done.

After that introduction, you're probably expecting a lecture on time management. I will indeed talk about learning as much as you can during the time available. But time keeps going—it can't be saved or managed as money can, even though people do speak of it as if it could. Books and lectures on time management usually propose sectioning days and weeks into blocks and assigning each to some activity. If people are really doing this, they are very quiet about it. Most people I know appear to be winging it, even those who get an enormous amount done.

Time-management methods sometimes give the impression that they can do the impossible: make learning automatic—something that *will* happen if you follow certain steps. Besides being unable to fulfill that implied promise, typical time-management methods seldom assume a realistic world—one that is typically disorderly. Our days are likely filled with events that are out of our control and often unpredictable. Time management tends to ignore the messiness of life. Even so, some people are dedicated to time management, and profit from the orderliness and organization it brings into their lives. If it works for you, by all means use it.

For the rest, you can get by without a time-management scheme, but you can't get far without discipline. If learning becomes a high-priority item, you'll get it done no matter what. If it doesn't, time management won't help.

To repeat, high-priority things always get done. For the successful student, reading and writing for courses were not things that got done only if other activities didn't use up all the time. On the contrary, learning had a higher priority than *other activities*. For the average new student just out of high school, getting priorities sorted out requires discipline. Even if you have made the firm decision that you're going to learn as much as you can in college, actually doing so means walking away from dorm bull sessions or the TV in order to do the necessary reading and writing. Remember, you can't lie about your priorities. Anyone who says learning has a high priority but never does any of it is fibbing, and it's obvious to everyone. You will demonstrate that you place a high priority on learning by spending a good part of your 40 unscheduled hours engaged with course material.

Somewhat exceptional students find eventually that discipline is not needed. Like the weight trainer who lifts because the very act of lifting, difficult as it is, has become satisfying in itself, some students discover that learning tickles the brain, and they no longer see it as a chore. Learning has become a hobby, and hobbies are always high-priority items.

Your Unscheduled Hours

One thing all new students should eliminate from their thinking is the notion that all unscheduled time between classes is "free" time. If your intent is to learn, a goodly part of your unscheduled time will have to be devoted to doing it. Here is a rough outline of the activities that have to be taken care of, on your own initiative, during unscheduled time:

1. Routine assignments
   a. Submitted
   b. Teacher-generated, not submitted
   c. Student-generated, not submitted

2. Nonroutine assignments
   a. Submitted
      i. Short papers
      ii. Long papers
   b. Not submitted

3. Review for exams

Routine Assignments

Routine assignments are usually associated with courses in mathematics, science, and engineering. Such courses present something of a paradox to students. Nearly everyone finds them intellectually challenging; but, at the same time, they are the least ambiguous when it comes to knowing what to do to learn the content. These subjects are best learned by working through characteristic problems of the discipline. For this reason, teachers of these subjects give assignments very regularly, sometimes every day. There is likely to be a quiz or a laboratory report due every week. So with a subject like thermodynamics (not exactly a walk in the park, by the way), there is no uncertainty about what needs to be done to learn it. Working out the answers to questions and problems is the way the subject is learned.

Math classes provide a clear example of routine submitted assignments. In fact, the prospect of five problems due, routinely, every class period for a year can be depressing if you dwell on it. The answer, then, is not to dwell on the total number of problems that will be done or the total time it will take. As the Chinese say, even the longest journey starts with a single step. Athletes remind us frequently that they play their games one at a time. Concentrate on one assignment only: the one that needs attention today.

Two ideas, taken to heart, can turn routine assignments into a part of your day that is as natural as taking a shower. First, routine assignments nearly always constitute practice at something that needs to become natural and comfortable. Routine assignments are like baseball practice. You keep repeating, adding new skills, and improving. Secondly, as in the case of baseball practice, a set time and environment gets you going, even on those days you just don't feel like it. Routine assignments can be done alone, preferably in some quiet nook in the library, and should be done free of distractions. You are most likely perfecting some skill, working out formulas, proving relationships, writing clear paragraphs, deducing new information from given data, and things of the sort. Such work requires an engaged mind. Your attention must be focused on what you are doing. No matter what you might claim, you cannot keep your attention focused with a TV or stereo playing loudly. You cannot concentrate in a cafeteria where hundreds of people are dropping silverware and talking and laughing loudly. It is possible, of course, to fill a page with words or figures even in the midst of the most severe distractions. This is what is known as "doing an assignment." This kind of "doing" is not much different from knitting or some other activity you can do absentmindedly. Assignments are for learning. "Doing" them without learning is a dreary way to use your time.

There is one very good idea from time-management methods that you may want to try. Find a wall calendar that has one full page for each month and a box you can write in for each day of the month. Routine assignments should become part of *your* routine as well. If you have a physics lab each Wednesday and a report due the following Wednesday, assign a fixed period each week for preparing the report, preferably just after the laboratory session and not just before the report is due. Mark your calendar every week for a couple of months and discipline yourself to do the lab report every week at the assigned time. Once it becomes part of your routine, things will take care of themselves. The calendar is also very good for keeping track of exam dates, due dates for longer assignments, book reports, and birthdays.

You can make routine assignments more interesting and profitable by having a working partner. Someone who shares your interest in learning the subject and is willing to meet regularly to do the assignments can be of enormous help. The help, in fact, is mutual. You help one another, for several reasons. Study partners motivate one another. Missing an assignment session means not only missing the assignment, but having let someone down as well. Most important, it buoys the spirit to have someone to talk to when you get stuck.

Be very careful about assignment sessions involving more than two people. These things have a way of degenerating into parties. Also, and it hardly needs saying, the point of it all is to learn and to teach one another when required; copying or exchanging answers defeats the whole purpose.

Far more demanding of discipline are the nonsubmitted assignments. For some, in fact, a nonsubmitted assignment is a weird beast indeed. A frightening number of freshmen enter college thinking, "Why do it if you don't get credit?" Here we are revisiting an old problem. Without the intent to learn, and a vision of courses as learning opportunities, college becomes a long ordeal of collecting credits earned through assignments and exams. If you read, write, and solve problems in order to learn, the benefit comes during the reading, writing, and problem solving. Whether the teacher or anyone else sees or grades the work becomes secondary. This will likely come as a shocking idea, so consider an analogous situation between a doctor and patient. It would be peculiar indeed for a patient to take medication only to please the doctor, or to stop taking it because the physician stopped checking up on him each visit to see whether he was following instructions. We follow a physician's suggestions because we believe the physician knows what will make us better. It should be much the same with teachers. Assignments are simply the way teachers tell students how to learn.

There are, without question, routine things that must be done to learn—things for which you do not receive credit—that a teacher never checks on. Sometimes teachers suggest these activities; sometimes you'll invent them yourself. The clearest and most obvious routine nonsubmitted assignment is reading. Teachers give reading lists, or assign (or sometimes only suggest) chapters or topics to be studied. The great danger is to miss the point that these are routine activities—to be done every day or every other day.

Learning something every day, through reading and writing (and talking), is not something that many new college students come prepared to do. Everyone agrees that they will need to study, but not everyone's experience has prepared them for this kind of study. I am hesitant to even use the word *study,* because it is so much misused and misunderstood. Study is far too often associated with exams—so much so that some students study *only* if there is an exam within the next two days. One of the worst things you can do is equate study with preparing for exams.

Study should really mean *learning*. Learning is done best when the thing to be learned is manageable and well defined. That means dealing with the content in small chunks. If it is true that mathematics is best learned by mastering each small segment as it comes up, why not use that tried and true formula for all courses? Consider a typical college biology text. Four chapters might be devoted to four subjects: digestion, circulation, respiration, and genetics. It might take the teacher six weeks to say what she has to say on those four topics. It simply is not realistic to believe that anyone could learn in two nights what a teacher has lectured on for six weeks and a writer took sixty pages to cover. Identical arguments can be made for the study of French, economics, and most

other disciplines. Consider the medical metaphor again. If someone were in-
structed to take two tablets every day, they would certainly not wait a month
and then take all sixty of them the night before their next appointment. The
analogy is indeed fanciful, but our mental systems can no more deal with sixty
pages of challenging material in one night than our physical systems could with
sixty pills.

Filling In the Notes

If doing teacher-generated but nonsubmitted assignments strikes you as a
novel idea, think about generating your own assignments. It sounds almost
heroic, but there is one self-generated assignment that comes quite naturally and is guaranteed to produce results. We might call it "filling in the
notes," just to have a name for it. As suggested earlier, interesting teachers
sometimes do not "give good notes." They say very important things and mention ideas that you really should know something about, but they may not produce a neat outline with each point annotated for easy learning. Your own
notes, under these conditions, might be skimpy and fragmented. Looking at
them later, you would realize that important things had been said during the
lecture, but what they were would not be obvious from the notes.

A good self-generated assignment, then, is to fill in your class notes some-
time before the next lecture. The most successful students do this almost routinely, like the math assignments that come every period. "Filling in" is not a
difficult job in most cases. It means using material from the reading list, from
the textbook, or from study partners, to convert words, phrases, lists, and
names into a meaningful picture. (Some teachers encourage this learning-in-
small-bits by presenting the class with unannounced "pop quizzes.")

A tutor who helps a new student frequently starts with the student's notebook. Often the tutor cannot tell from the notes what the teacher wanted the
student to know. Words, phrases, and diagrams are there, but there are no
ideas. The notes do not provide answers to the *how* and *why* questions that are
at the heart of any discipline. A good way to start the filling-in process is to
generate complete sentences that state relationships. We all overestimate our
ability to reconstruct ideas from a few words. Key words alone seldom trigger
any useful idea in our heads, yet our first attempts at serious note making are
all too often just clusters of key words. A biology student with the words "hemoglobin—blood" in his notebook was unable to construct a sentence that
stated the true relationship between the two words. A tutor had to spend some
time filling in relationships for the student. She had to tell him that about half
the volume of blood consisted of red cells (erythrocytes), that hemoglobin was
a protein, that hemoglobin was found only inside the red cells, and that it was
the hemoglobin that accepted and held on to oxygen. Without tutorial help,

the student knew only that there was some relationship between blood and hemoglobin, and could not say what it was. A major point here is that the student in this example would have learned a great deal more by discovering this relationship on his own than by listening to someone else say it. In fact, everything the tutor said had already been said by the teacher during the lecture, which proves that just hearing something and jotting down key words is not enough to cause learning. Your notes need to have *verbs*—words that show action or state clearly the relationship between things. You need sentences!

Making real sentences out of words and phrases, in the case of a new or challenging topic, usually requires help. That does not mean a tutor is required. Help is always at hand in books. That student who could not state clearly the relationship between hemoglobin and blood could have looked up hemoglobin in the index of his textbook. Any worthwhile biology textbook will have a paragraph or two on hemoglobin, stating just what it is, where it is, and what it does. It is not enough, however, to just read the words. "Filling in" notes means making a permanent record, in your own hand, of what you have just learned. It is also a good idea to paraphrase what you have read and not just copy the words. Learning means thinking, and paraphrasing is both a cause and a test of thinking.

I do not believe there is any study activity that is more productive than using books and other sources to convert class notes to solid ideas expressed in clear sentences.

Nonroutine Assignments

Assignments and other learning events that come up only once or a few times each semester or term might be called nonroutine. These include papers of varying length, term papers, book reports, and the like, all of which are normally submitted for examination and grading. You may also be asked to do fairly extensive research in preparation for a class discussion, a presentation, or a debate. Such preparation would be evaluated, most likely, but might not be submitted.

The short writing assignment is a marvelous way to learn a well-defined topic. However, such assignments still present only an opportunity for learning and no guarantee. As noted in the case of the more routine assignment, these can also be "done" with little or no learning. "Using" assignments instead of "doing" them involves, again, a certain mindset or attitude at the beginning.

The very word *assignment* sets the wrong tone. In the ideal classroom, the teacher would *suggest* to students that research, reading, or paraphrasing certain passages or books would enable them to better understand the subject. This is the way people who are no longer in school (but continue to learn) choose the things they read: from among suggestions or recommendations they get from friends and book reviews. But our habits begin to gel when we are children, and when we were in the early grades few of us could see the point of school except as organized play. We could not be expected to comprehend the importance of learning. At that time in our lives, mere *suggestions* tend to be ignored unless they involve doing something that is fun. To repeat our theme, learning satisfies a deep biological need, but one that is quite distinct from the need for fun. Still, teachers of the early grades try (with hardly any success) to convince fifth-graders that compound fractions are fun. The kids see through that immediately and teachers have to "play the homework card."

Homework is a fine and necessary thing when the work assigned has the *potential* for facilitating learning. Over the years, however, it has become busy-work, assigned out of habit or routine. More often than not, students do it only because it is required for "credit" or a grade.

So first-time college students can bring to this new and extraordinary learning opportunity a cynical and unpleasant attitude toward *homework* and therefore toward its college counterpart, the assignment. You will help yourself enormously by abandoning any notion that assignments are punishment. Start all your courses with the attitude that assignments are good suggestions for learning and are, therefore, to be "used" and not merely "done" for credit.

My earlier general suggestions on writing are applicable to assignments as well. One in particular bears repeating, particularly for nonroutine assignments: Don't do them in one sitting. Most emphatically, don't schedule your work by calculating backward from the due date. One of Murphy's Laws is that the work always runs out just after the time allotted to do it. Planning to do the writing in the last four available hours before the paper is due is inviting disaster.

As I have already written at some length about learning and writing, what I will address here is primarily the matter of getting down to doing what has already been described. Even so, following the suggestion that writing assignments not be attempted in one sitting will improve the quality of the work done (and so the learning), as well as ensure that the assignment will be ready for submission on the due date.

Procrastination

Undiscovered in our complement of genes is one, I am sure, that provides great pleasure to our psyches when we find ourselves with nothing that needs doing. This hypothetical gene probably started out as a reward for a successful hunt or something of the sort. Contentment fairly wells up within us when we find that we do not have to do anything for a while. It's easy, then, to have good feelings toward the teacher who does not have an assignment due before the third week of class. But, quite obviously, the time gap between the giving of the assignment and its due date has a more serious purpose. The intent is to provide the student an opportunity to "handle" the assignment material several times. Note that handling the material several times is not at all the same as merely stretching out the writing process, or doing the assignment early to get it out of the way. Try the following method on a few assignments: The same day your first assignment is announced, get a simple folder with pockets that will be used only for assignments in that particular course. Within 24 hours after the assignment is announced, start collecting information. This is not at all difficult and requires very little time, but it is most important to start the same day or the next. During an hour between classes, find some books, start a bibliography, read a chapter and make some notes, or do the "incomplete-statements" trick suggested in Chapter 6, "Writing." The point is to get something specific about that assignment into the folder. Doing just a half hour's reading, or putting together a half page of notes, has the effect of getting the brain active—something like planting the seeds for the final product. A few days later, during one of your 40 unscheduled hours, take out the folder and add something to it—notes on another few pages of reading, maybe an outline of the way you think the paper will develop, or start the "beginning, middle, and end" layout suggested in Chapter 6, "Writing," or make a short list of questions that need answering before you can actually start writing.

After a few of these work sessions, which need be no longer than half an hour, the contents of the folder will be familiar to you. A minute's review, and you are ready to add to your growing body of information and reflections on the topic. If you have been thinking about the content material through all this and not just rewriting words, you will begin to feel not only comfortable with the topic, but perhaps even like something of an expert. In truth, getting to feel like an expert is the real point of using a folder, spreading the collection over several days, and keeping written notes. No one feels comfortable with new information the first time they encounter it. Confidence comes with repeated exposure, and the exposures need not be lengthy to have the desired effect. The important thing seems to be that there be some time between the exposures.

By the time you actually begin writing the assignment, you should know pretty much what you are going to say. Don't begin writing until you *have* become something of an expert. Having the topic well in hand before starting to write is not, in fact, the way most beginners proceed. More commonly, new information flows into the first draft (or even the final one) the instant it is discovered. The paper simply grows—sentence by sentence—as new things are added on at the end. People who write this way are likely to have forgotten what they wrote at the top of the page by the time they get to the bottom.

Worse, the "information" transcribed may well have activated the visual and motor parts of the brain without disturbing the thinking parts; in other words, the writing has not involved thinking.

Writing, you recall, has two primary purposes in college: learning and evaluation. If you collect and organize information in short sessions spread over a number of days, much of the first purpose, learning, is achieved by the time you are ready to write. The actual writing of the work to be submitted is just to show the world what you have learned.

Longer Assignments

Term papers or book reports require considerably more time and effort than short papers, but the approach used for short papers is also applicable to longer efforts. As in virtually all serious learning, the making of clear notes is absolutely essential. As reading, note making, and writing have all been considered in previous chapters, we now need treat only the mechanics of actually getting all this done during unscheduled time. The critical aspect of the process is not to try to eat the whole mattress in one sitting.

Teachers often find a small increase in the number of empty seats in their classrooms toward the end of a semester. This happens because a number of students are coming up on end-of-semester exams or term-paper due dates in other courses, and are cutting all their classes, using that time to study or do the term paper. This is surely a case of short-circuiting the learning process. Besides which, an assignment or exam preparation postponed so long that classes must be cut to do it becomes sheer grinding toil.

Starting work on a long paper on the Tuesday before a Friday due date is going to put the procrastinator in a foul mood, and with good reason. The simple truth is that nearly everyone finds totally unfamiliar topics tedious or uninteresting, or even boring. The problem here is not biological. We hear from a variety of sources that young people have short attention spans—a matter of a few minutes. There is no truth in this strange claim. Certainly young people cannot tolerate being bored for long periods of time, but that is true of everyone. College-age students have no difficulty concentrating on quite challenging material for 40 or 50 minutes. The real problem is trying to spend long periods of time struggling with something that is *not yet interesting.*

At one time (if I may be allowed a personal example) I had no patience with psychological studies on the physiology of perception in cats. I found it hard to imagine why anyone would care. In preparation for writing this book, however, I dipped my toe into the cold waters of cognitive science—a field of study concerned with what the brain is doing, and how it is changed, during the process of learning. The arcane and previously uninteresting area of neurophysiology quickly took on new importance. Eventually I found myself fascinated by articles on visual perception—and not really surprised by that turn of events. A little curiosity, combined with a need to know, is all it takes to focus attention and get the brain going. Interest will follow as day follows night.

In the case of writing a longish paper, then, the very first investigations into the topic might not arouse any interest. If that is the case, why would anyone want to stretch the very first encounter to 5 or 6 hours? A new thing needs time, time to meander around in the subconscious, to ferment. Procrastinators rationalize their last-minute efforts by claiming that they work better under pressure. What this really means is that nothing short of simple terror in the face of a deadline can motivate them to get down to it. But the experiment that demonstrates the counterproductiveness of compressing a task into a fixed period has already been done. Psychologists set people to work with the instruction that they were to work every day for a fixed period of time, with no requirements as to the amount of work to be accomplished. Later, they changed the instruction so that the workers had to do a certain amount of work, but there was no specified length of time they had to spend doing it. In both cases, the work done was about the same, the work was well done, and the workers were content with their jobs. The conditions were changed a third time to specify that a certain amount of work had to be done *and* it had to be done within a specified period of time. Under these conditions, the workers became irritable, morale dropped, and the quality of their work deteriorated. The first two cases involved pressure-free conditions. The workers only had to work 8 hours, with no demands that they get a certain amount done, or else they worked until the required task was done with no limitations on how quickly or how slowly they worked. Only a condition like a *double bind*—requirements on both the work to be done and the time in which it must be done—caused the workers to become cranky and dissatisfied.

It is clear that students who start an assignment so close to the due date that there is going to be no time at all to dawdle have put themselves into this kind of double bind. It's almost impossible to work efficiently with one eye on the clock and worrying almost constantly: "Is this going to get done in time?" Certainly not much learning will get done.

The two purposes of the assignment, learning and evaluation, are nearly always closely linked. Most assignments are evaluated with an eye for correctness and clarity of expression and coherence. Experienced readers can distinguish almost immediately between a paper that presents an overall coherent picture, and a sequence of statements that are all individually correct but collectively fail to convey useful information. It is not possible to write a coherent and instructive paper without knowing well what it is you are talking about. It follows that the evaluation (grade) tracks very closely with the amount of learning that went on during the preparation for the actual writing, which is exactly as it should be. Conversely, an assignment can be "done," in the sense of filling several pages with statements from various sources, without learning much about the topic, but this will almost certainly be detected by an alert reader and the evaluation will suffer.

Nonsubmitted Assignments

At a high level of academic accomplishment, learning is done for the sheer sake of knowing something. A small step below this is learning for the sake of being able to talk intelligently to someone else about the matter. Teachers know that the ability to speak intelligently about a topic is a satisfying—and profitable—skill. They do you a great favor by suggesting practice.

Specific assignments that are not submitted are more common in courses in literature, the humanities, and the social sciences; they frequently take the form of readings in preparation for a classroom discussion or debate. The way you go about preparing nonsubmitted assignments will determine whether or not you attain the goal they intend. A common approach is to read what was assigned and hope you can retain enough to answer whatever questions come up. You will remember, however, the suggestions in Chapter 5, "Reading": Just reading does not fix things in the mind. It is paraphrasing and writing that focus the mind and give the brain a workout. So even if nothing is to be handed in, learning goes on. Passages must be read and paraphrased, and, we will now see, *talked about.*

Talking

Whether you are working on submitted assignments, nonsubmitted assignments, exam preparation, or class notes, one of the best learning techniques, and one of the most neglected, is *talking.* Speaking is the most obvious and familiar way we deal with language. Much of our speech does not, however, concern itself with intellectually challenging material. Most of the time we talk about what we have done or want to do, what we like, or how we feel about one thing or another. Talking is something we do effortlessly, it seems, until a teacher calls on us.

What happens when a teacher asks you to summarize the events and the environment that prompted Tom Wolfe to write *The Painted Word,* or review the comparison of *Brave New World* and *1984* that Neil Postman used to begin *Amusing Ourselves to Death?* Typically, what happens is that the brain freezes up, panic sets in, and we shrug or begin making up a story from bits and scraps of what we can remember. A quick reading will not prepare you to launch into a meaningful discussion of either of these topics. Making notes would, of course, help enormously, but talking about it all in advance would help even more. So how do you do that?

You do it by gathering a few classmates for a study session. It takes a fair amount of discipline for several people to get together for study and stick to it, particularly for a reading assignment. But if you are disciplined, you can turn a group reading session into a terrific preparation for a classroom discussion. The secret is to talk to one another about the reading you have been assigned and question one another on it. To be effective, the questions must be serious, meaning that they must be much like those you can expect when the classroom discussion takes place. A question such as "Who wrote *Brave New World?*" falls into the category of trivia: It's not the kind of question that evokes any deeper understanding, either of *Brave New World* or of its importance to the arguments of Neil Postman. You should be trying instead to reconstruct and paraphrase Postman's thinking. You should be asking one another why Postman chose those two books in the first place. What do they have in common, how are they different, and how do Postman's arguments flow from these similarities and differences?

You should not be puzzled by disagreements within the study group or shy away from them. You are not trying to come up with a list of "right answers." The point of questioning and arguing is to practice putting ideas into words. A half-baked idea reveals its flaws only when it is put into words. By the same token, a vague and uncertain notion of the writer's intent can become progressively clearer as members of the group paraphrase the original text. A consensus may or may not emerge, but lasting and useful changes will have occurred in the brain. Conceptions or opinions are likely to be repeated a number of times and rephrased to sharpen their precision. You are struggling with the language—and you can only win.

You can easily imagine the new and confident frame of mind you would bring to a classroom discussion the day after you and your group had spent an hour verbalizing and sharpening your understanding of a writer's intent. The night before was a dress rehearsal for the discussion period. If you then participate in the discussion (and how could you resist if you had all these insights to contribute?), you will learn still more and your understanding of Postman's thinking will be further refined to the extent that you may well indeed consider yourself something of an expert on this topic.

What I have described above, a small group in serious fact-based discussion about a nontrivial topic, is learning of the highest kind. You are doing exactly the *kind* of thing the keenest and best-developed intellects do when they are most focused. The only difference between you and them is a matter of experience and of the size of the respective databases. More experienced learners simply know more things because they have read more, thought more, and talked more. They are more persuasive in their discussions because they have larger vocabularies and are more practiced at putting ideas into words. But they got that way by doing exactly what I am suggesting you do; they were not born with those skills or that information already in their heads.

Exams

Exams and other forms of testing will be treated in detail later, but, since most of the preparation goes on between classes, a word is in order here about spending some of your unscheduled time getting ready for exams. It is obvious by now that there are many things to be done between classes in order to learn as much as you can in college. There will always be a few students, however, who believe that studying for exams is the *only* thing that needs doing between classes. This is probably the gravest mistake that new college students make. Nevertheless, exams are going to come and they need to be prepared for.

The best way of preparing for exams combines three ideas I have already discussed. First, do what has been suggested earlier to prepare for a written assignment: Make notes; review them frequently; add new information each time. Second, verbalize and work in small groups as if preparing for a performance. Finally, don't do it all in one sitting.

From this chapter and from Chapter 4, "Attending Class," it becomes clear that learning goes on both during the 15 or so hours a week you spend in class and the 40 or so unscheduled hours you have between classes. It is equally obvious that learning does not just happen. One of my favorite writers, Jacques Barzun, says that there are no puzzling unsolved problems regarding learning (and teaching). What needs to be done in order to teach well and to learn has long since been discovered. When teaching and learning are not done well, it is not from lack of knowing how, but from an unwillingness to discipline ourselves and exert the effort it takes. Gathering material and making notes for assignments or exams weeks in advance means doing something that puts the brain through its paces. Like lifting weights or practicing the cello, it often means doing a difficult thing when it would be much more comfortable to watch TV, party, or hang out. *Discipline* is an old-fashioned word, often associated with cranks, but no one ever got good at anything without it.

eight

Strategies

Student Voices

I WOULD HAVE DIED WITHOUT MY STUDY GROUP!

—BETH

he word *strategy* carries implications of long-term, large-scale planning, as opposed to quick decisions made in the heat of battle. The word also suggests a certain element of scheming—some clever moves to outwit an enemy. Both connotations fit our purposes here. In college many situations will pop up that require you to cope, and it helps to be quick-witted and to be able to make decisions on the run. However, it's not a good idea to bank entirely on your presumed ability to react quickly and wisely. An overall strategy will reduce the number of occasions for hectic reactive scrambling; the fewer of these, the better.

Is there an enemy, then? Against whom or what do we scheme? Walt Kelly's cartoon character Pogo found an answer when he said, "We have met the enemy and he is us." The college personnel—teachers, administrators, librarians, and so on—are certainly not enemies of students. Nor is it the purpose of regulations to thwart your academic progress. When there is a struggle or a fight, it is against a wrong attitude, a lack of discipline, lethargy, or procrastination; we are our own worst enemies in matters of learning. Having a strategy will mean formulating certain courses of action that are generally applicable in many situations and anticipate our all-too-human tendency to let things slide.

Most good learning practices would qualify as strategies if they are adopted in advance and become habits of the mind. The suggestions I made earlier concerning reading, writing, attending class, using assignments and unscheduled time between classes, and reviewing for exams are specific approaches to general academic challenges, and so might be considered strategies. But now we should consider the somewhat more subtle aspects of the academic life in college and some broader and longer-range strategies.

Attitude Revisited

The recurring message of this book is that learning is not the automatic result of performing certain prescribed behaviors. Nor is it something that happens to you; it is something you do consciously and intentionally to your brain. To learn, you must intend to remake yourself—to be other than you were before. Clearly, then, the grand overreaching strategy is to be an active participant in all the learning situations you will encounter.

That you become an active participant in your own education is the best advice anyone could give, but for some students it's the hardest to receive. Active participation includes asking questions or contributing to group discussions. Now, for every person who loves being the center of attention, there are several who hate and fear it. If you are one of the latter, you will want to use a trick or two to get over self-consciousness. Shyness is not biological or genetic. An exceptionally fine marching-band drum major I once knew was a shy lad with a stutter. He was self-conscious in normal classroom and social situations and spoke, haltingly, as little as possible. When asked how he could become so bold, forceful, and articulate on the marching field, he said that all he could think about out there was keeping eighty people together and getting them from point A to point B. In short, total preoccupation with the task at hand absorbed his consciousness; there was nothing left over for thinking about himself. Similarly, it's almost impossible to be angry and embarrassed at the same time. Anger directs consciousness away from the self and toward the cause of the anger. The mind cannot focus on more than one thing at a time.

I strongly suspect that a searing need to know, to understand, or to get to the bottom of some problem can take over the consciousness to such an extent that self-consciousness is not possible. Shy people do brave things when the problem at hand takes over the mind. So, again, we see the importance of attitude. When the need to know and the process of learning become paramount, they preoccupy consciousness. The eager learners forget self and plunge into debate, discussion, and argument. They still claim they're shy, but you'd never know it.

Getting Connected

When Harvard seniors and graduates were asked about their college experience, those who found it highly successful—both gratifying and educational—were in extraordinarily close agreement about one thing: They associated their academic success with getting connected with a group of students (sometimes graduate students) and with faculty. These were not social groups—at least that was not their primary purpose. Such groups sprang up around certain courses or academic disciplines. Many got started because students were impressed by their teachers, who were, in many cases, the brightest and most knowledgeable people those students had ever met. They began hanging around after class to pick these people's brains. They met like-minded classmates. They found they were welcome in the office, lab, or studio, and that it was not considered unusual for undergraduates to talk things over with teachers. These informal encounters were the seeds of study groups, and the involved students found themselves suddenly, and often for the first time in their lives, intensely interested in matters of the mind.

Getting connected in this way was the factor most frequently cited as contributing to academic satisfaction for the many hundreds of students and graduates interviewed. Clearly, then, your second broad strategy for college should be to get connected with faculty and other learning students. Now, if you are typical, your first impulse (based possibly on previous experience) would be to do just the opposite—to sit quietly in class and not cause trouble, and to study quietly in the library with no one around to bother you. But the experiment has already been done; the quiet isolationist approach is not the one that works.

Finding or starting a biology study group, or bugging your psychology teacher, probably sounds like a nerdy thing to do. But the "conventional wisdom"—that most students are in college to party, and that faculty want nothing to do with undergraduates—is simply wrong. The relatively few students who take advantage of their new freedom get a lot of press, and so give the impression that they are representative of undergraduates. A few aloof faculty members have likewise had an effect disproportionate to their numbers. The truth is that most students would like to learn and most teachers would like to help. To make it happen you simply have to take charge of matters. Find congenial teachers and like-minded classmates and make it happen.

Study Groups

You are likely to have been advised, at one time or another, to become involved in extracurricular activities. The Harvard studies did show a generally higher degree of overall satisfaction with the college experience among those who were involved in some extracurricular activity such as publications, volunteer work, student senate, or intramural sports. But such activities did not correlate well with academic success, meaning that they neither increased nor diminished academic achievement. In fact, spending as much as 20 hours a week at work (paid or unpaid), sports, or other nonacademic activities had no effect on either grades or learning. Both grades and learning were reduced, however, among those who tried to learn in isolation and did all their studying alone. If learning is "languaging," practice with the language is essential. To practice, you need other people. There is no need, then, to discover on your own what your predecessors have already found out: that a most useful occasion to exercise the language—and so to learn—is the small group.

Advisors

The remarkable variability that exists within a faculty was taken up in Chapter 3, "Teachers." Learning how to discern various types, and to cope when that is necessary, should be a part of your long-term strategy. There is also the problem of knowing which are the good courses, or perhaps what is the *real* reputation of a certain department. How can you get the important and unpublished information about the college and its teachers? Having a confederate "on the inside" would help, and most colleges provide just such an opportunity by assigning the student an academic advisor.

In some institutions, advising is completely centralized in an advising office. Sometimes the advisors are full-time professionals who are not members of the teaching faculty. In other places, there is no centralized system and teaching faculty do all the advising in their offices. You may encounter an intermediate system, or combinations of these systems, in your school. Most schools will get you started by assigning an advisor. Like brokered marriages, these arrangements sometimes work out wonderfully and sometimes not at all. No matter what college you attend, it should have an uncomplicated way for you to change academic advisors if you wish to do so. If not, that should be the first order of business for the student senate.

Giving students their own faculty member or professional advisor was a stroke of genius. Life will be smoother if you take maximum advantage of the system. Advisors who have been on campus a while are veritable storehouses of useful information, opinions, and even gossip. At the very least, they can direct you to sources of reliable information.

The primary sources of information are people and print. Don't rely exclusively on either. No one person knows everything, and printed documents about various disciplines are sometimes more persuasive than informative. One of your strategies should be to know as much as possible about courses, teachers, and disciplines before you commit yourself. After the first or second semester you will have a lot of discretion in such matters. You will, in fact, design your own schedule. There may be four different teachers of French in a given semester, and their courses offered at various times of the day. Making an informed choice at the beginning is far better than trying to rearrange a schedule after the semester is under way.

You may also find that the major you thought you wanted is not at all what you anticipated. A very large number of students change their majors, sometimes twice or three times. Changing majors is no disgrace and is in no way a sign of failure. Picking a major is a little like going on a blind date. It's not a commitment for life. No one would continue a relationship that had all the earmarks of disaster; similarly, you would not discontinue a relationship only because it started out by chance. The situation is similar with the major. How you get into it is much less important than how it suits you. If it doesn't suit you, consider a change.

Because entering students seldom have really sufficient understanding of the various disciplines, some colleges no longer allow freshmen to declare a major. In these schools, freshmen take a year of coursework that will be generally useful no matter what the future holds. During that year, they are encouraged to find out all they can about the disciplines at the institution. They do this by taking a course or two in a discipline that interests them, by reading, and primarily by talking to upper-level students and faculty. An academic advisor is a good place to start.

Advice, remember, is not the same as instruction. All decisions regarding courses, teachers, and majors are decisions of the student and not the advisor. Responsibility in these matters cannot be transferred. Advice is best thought of as information.

New students who have previously depended on someone else to make the decisions (in a few cases, even which college to attend!) might become exasperated with an advisor who describes courses and teachers and relates college or departmental requirements, but never actually *tells* the student what to do. That, however, is exactly what advice is: information to help you choose wisely. It follows that you will want an advisor who is well informed. Charm, wit, friendliness, and physical attractiveness cannot compensate for misinformation. Even though the responsibility is ultimately theirs, many students will still rely on advisors to tell them about requirements for graduation and other academic regulations. Imagine the state you'd be in if you discovered during your last semester that you could not graduate because you had not fulfilled a literature or language requirement. A *knowledgeable* advisor is likely to catch these things before it's too late.

Academic advisors can make an enormous difference in the course of your education. If they are experienced and well connected, they can suggest the better courses or better teachers, enumerate all the pros and cons of choosing or changing your major, direct you to various services such as tutoring or workshops in word processing, help set up study groups, remind you regularly of requirements, and, when that's needed, listen to your problems.

Remember two things about advice. It's terrific for preventing problems and not good at all for getting you out of jams. And it can be disastrous when it's based on misinformation. There was the young woman who dropped her Spanish class because she heard at a party that "they" were going to discontinue the requirement for a foreign language; or the lad who failed a required history course because he heard that attending the class was not mandatory.

Half a minute with a competent academic advisor would have prevented these minor catastrophes, but no amount of talking can undo them after the fact.

Your academic advisor need not, and should not, be your only faculty contact. Another myth the Harvard study dispelled was that of "inaccessible faculty." Students who enjoyed a satisfying and profitable educational experience reported that they found the large majority of faculty happy to meet with them and discuss whatever they wanted. These sessions were particularly rewarding because of the tendency of faculty to interact with students as adults and not as children (recall the consideration of this point in Chapter 3, "Teachers"). Those students who believed that most of the faculty were seldom on campus, or too busy to talk with students, had gotten that impression from "student talk"—they themselves had never tried to arrange a visit with a faculty member. Frequent contact with faculty—advisors and others—should be part of your long-term strategy.

Gender-Specific Strategies

Academic progress, and academic problems, are not remarkably different for the two sexes. In two small areas, however, there is a history of the behavior or expectations of men and women being statistically different. Studies have shown that male students who experienced difficulties or fell short of their goals tended to look toward circumstances or outside events as causes. In similar situations, women more frequently perceived their own lack of effort or persistence as the cause. Men tended to value knowledge and experience in advisors and faculty contacts, whereas women looked more for friendliness and personal interest. A small part of the men's strategy, therefore, might be to resolve to accept more responsibility for the course of their academic career. Women, on the other hand, might want to spend some time looking for the right advisor, or perhaps have more than one.

Taking Charge

One of the more unsettling aspects of college for the new student is an apparent lack of concern for the individual student—at times a lack of awareness even. There was the freshman who got the course schedule for a junior psychology major who happened to have the same name. The junior who got the freshman schedule had dropped the wrong classes and added the correct ones by the end of the first day. The freshman sat glassy-eyed through bewildering lectures for a week, waiting for somebody to do something. Again, you cannot let college be something that happens *to* you. The institution should be seen as a large and complex system of almost unlimited possibilities for both good and bad. It can roll over you and grind you up if you let it. Your strategy should be to make an ally out of complexity. The bigger and more disorganized a system, the easier it is to use it to your advantage. Of course, doing so is only possible if you become active and take control of your academic career. If the faculty controls the drop/add system in your college, for example, there is no need to stay in a course with a teacher who mumbles and can't be heard beyond the second row. Find another section at a time you're free and add it, then drop the other section. (Always add first, then drop. Teachers may be required to let you drop their course, but they are not required to let you add it.)

Only if you know the system will you be able to determine the course of your academic life and lower the probability that things will simply happen to you. Part of your strategy should be to learn the system. In a typical college, that is no small task. A survey of the catalog (your best source for general information) will reveal dozens of organizations, groups, programs, and facilities for tutoring, work-study, off-campus credit, counseling, library help, computer workshops, and all the extracurricular activities and clubs on campus. It should have information on majors, academic rules, faculty lists, requirements, and ways to find people. There are some people, however, you have to find on your own. These are the helpful secretaries. Secretaries who know the system and like students are treasures. They can do wondrous things.

There is much to learn. Who are the good teachers who love their area of expertise and want me to know all about it? How many courses can I drop before the dean puts me on probation? Is there anyone who will read and critique my psych paper before I write the final draft? Does it cost anything to get tutoring in chemistry? How can I change academic advisors? Is help available in the library if I need it? Can I request a review if I feel I've been treated unfairly? How do I change my major?

The only consistently reliable sources of information are the official publications of the college. Rules and regulations can be found in the catalog, the student handbook, the admissions bulletin, and other printed material distributed by college offices. Other students are a notoriously bad source of information on such matters. Be wary any time you hear the words "They said." Do not make any decision based on "word-of-mouth" advice until you have checked it against official sources. Even academic advisors can be mistaken as to what constitutes a literature course or how humanities requirements for science majors need to be distributed across the disciplines. College administrators, on the other hand, can be very hard-nosed about these matters. They are not likely to excuse you from taking a required course because someone said, mistakenly, that it was not a requirement.

Official publications, then, are good sources for learning the rules and regulations. They are of no help, however, in trying to determine quality. Officially, everything the college offers is the finest available, but you would do well to find more disinterested sources for evaluating quality. We find here another of those curious little paradoxes. Official publications are the most reliable sources for matters of fact—rules, regulations, and requirements—but offer no help in matters of opinion—what's good or of high quality. Students, on the other hand, and most faculty, will give their honest opinions about programs, courses, and services, but may sometimes get the facts garbled in matters of rule.

In this regard, a word about unofficial or underground student publications is in order. At some colleges, students have taken it upon themselves to publish opinions on the quality of the institution's services—most notably of the teaching. Some of these publications are extraordinarily good; some are equally bad. There are few more difficult tasks than trying to make an objective evaluation of teaching. One's sense of comfort or discomfort in a classroom tends to lodge in the mind and can easily supplant a serious consideration of the long-term effects of the teaching. It's the good teachers, after all, who are least likely to let students get too comfortable. A course that preoccupies the mind may be seen as a bit of a nuisance while you're taking it. For such reasons, the most reliable student evaluations are those that come a year or more after the students took the courses. Courses that instill a love of literature or an appreciation of history, or that improve writing, or prepare the student for further continued learning, are all good courses even if they were an annoyance at the time they were taken.

Student publications that evaluate teachers need to be read, then, with care. Look for specific details as to what the teacher actually does. Don't trust a booklet that relies on punchy, one-word characterizations. *Super, terrific, dull,* or *jerk* gives you nothing but the gut reaction of a few students on a particular day. Don't avoid a teacher because he's characterized as a crank or gives difficult tests. Always look for something specific that suggests the course is or is not a good learning experience. A teacher who gives frequent quizzes or assignments and returns the results quickly is a good sign. "Wastes your time" or "Can't stick to the subject" are not good signs. Look also for a statement of the number of students reporting on a course. A report based on two student interviews does not become reliable because it appears in print. You'd do as well to ask your roommate.

Now and again you'll find a faculty member who has been around a while, has talked with lots of students, knows many of her colleagues, and is willing to give you her honest opinion. Some students, having found such a teacher, will check with her every semester to be sure they are getting the best courses consistent with their program and college requirements.

There are some quite specific elements of teaching methodology to look for—things that students have, in large numbers, found to be most helpful. Serious students want quick, or even instant, feedback on their efforts. For written assignments this is seldom possible, but in the case of exams they would like a set of acceptable answers as soon as possible after the exam, while the questions, and their own responses, are fresh in their minds. They like a short quiz at the end of a period to check their understanding. They like teachers who encourage them to talk in class and clear up any misconceptions immediately, before they have time to get lodged in long-term memory. Good students want to learn as much as they can in the classroom, through talking, through writing, and through instant feedback to find out whether their thinking is correct. They also appreciate having their writing evaluated *before* the final draft is submitted for grading.

Admittedly, it's no easy thing to dig out this sort of information about teachers. But it's worth the effort to try. Talk to people. Talk to upperclassmen (not just one) who have had the teacher you want to know about; talk to other teachers. Eavesdrop on study groups; ask questions about the courses they have taken; listen.

Grading

Always on the mind, even if only somewhere in the back, are grades. Grades have to be a part of strategy, but they can't be allowed to direct the whole show. If you made grades your highest priority, you would be forced to take the most simple-minded "gut" courses you could find. That, however, would make your high grade point average a hollow achievement, with no long-term benefit to you. It would also bore you to death. Your priorities should be: (1) Get the best teachers and courses; (2) learn as much as you can; (3) get the highest grades possible consistent with (1) and (2).

Assuming that you are in a good course and have set out to learn all you can, is there any strategy for getting high grades? As before, getting information right at the beginning is the first step. Learn each teacher's grading system. The college will have a uniform system for *reporting* grades, such as the A, B, C system, or the percentage system, or the four-point system, but teachers virtually always have complete control over how a grade is *determined*. The only consistent requirements are that each teacher's system be fair, comprehensible, and the same for all students. So some teachers put a letter grade on every piece of student work, and at the end use a formula to determine what one C, one C-minus, two B-minuses, and one A add up to. Others use percentage grades on all work and simply average them. Some use weighted percent grades, so that long papers or the final exam will contribute more toward the final grade. Another variation is the point system, in which a maximum number of possible points is assigned to each graded item and final grades are based on the number of points accumulated.

If a teacher has said nothing about the grading system by the end of the second week of classes, you would do well to hang around after class and tactfully suggest that the grading system be explained. There could be some surprises. A few teachers, for example, use a contract system for grading. This system might be encountered in studio courses, in some laboratories, and occasionally in literature. In a contract system, a grade is assigned for a specific number of reports submitted, drawings completed, or stories reviewed. Assuming acceptable quality, an A grade is guaranteed if the maximum number of items is submitted, with intermediate and low grades for correspondingly fewer items submitted.

Whatever its merits, the contract system elicits strong feelings among both students and teachers. Students who like it are spirited in their support. There is never any uncertainty in this system. The student knows from the beginning what must be done to earn an A or a B. (Such courses seldom have traditional exams.) Teachers who use the system admit that it uncouples grades from learning, but do not find that objectionable. Holding that measuring learning is arbitrary and subjective (in the specific areas in question), they have chosen not to pretend that they are able to make such a determination. Instead, they require certain work that has the *potential* for facilitating appreciation and understanding, and therefore learning. They accept that students can get good grades without learning much, but claim, with considerable justification, that such students hurt only themselves by not taking advantage of a learning situation.

Teachers who use contract learning take the very high ground in the grading/learning debate. They grade on the basis of whether or not the students availed themselves of the opportunities provided, and leave the actual learning or appreciation in the hands of the students.

Some students and faculty oppose contract grading as strongly as others favor it. They hold that if the evaluation of learning is arbitrary and subjective for the teacher, it is still more so for the student. Many students want feedback from the teacher; they feel they are less competent than teachers at judging progress or clear thinking. They would like grades that reflect, even if imperfectly, their level of progress or understanding.

This small digression serves to point up just one element in the ongoing debate on grades. More important, it reminds you that it is to your advantage to know as early as possible how grades are determined, or generated, in your courses. You should certainly find out whether attendance will affect your grade or your status in a course. The idea here is not to encourage cutting, but to advise you to find out in advance what the consequences will be if you want to cut for any reason.

When it comes to learning in advance about assignments and exams, things get tricky. Knowing *nothing* about a teacher's exams, or the way he evaluates assignments, doesn't seem like a good idea. On the other hand, too great a preoccupation with those things can misdirect your efforts toward pleasing the teacher, when your real concern should be the subject matter. In the best situations, it will make no difference. If you learn well and write well, your assignments and performance on exams will reflect this, and an open-minded and sensitive teacher will grade you accordingly. Should you come across a teacher who has in mind precisely what he expects to see in an assignment, or who wants to find only his own words and opinions on an exam, then you have little choice but to do what's expected. If you learn about this early enough, you might consider taking a section with a different teacher.

Sources of some controversy are the "files" on teachers. Well-organized dorms, clubs, scholarly societies, fraternities, and sororities are likely to have stored somewhere boxes of old exams, book reports, themes, and term papers assigned by those teachers who have a reputation for challenging students. Although not all teachers agree with me on this point, I consider such files to be completely ethical and suggest you use them when they are available. A student's work is his own possession, and if he chooses to share it with others, he is simply following the practice of a long line of scholars. The question here is how to make best use of such a windfall of data. To read and study someone else's work in preparation for writing a paper is learning at its best. But to merely retype someone else's words and submit them as one's own is both unethical and illegal. It's called plagiarism, and is grounds for failure—or even dismissal—in some schools. Equally serious, the plagiarist has squandered a terrific learning opportunity and turned it into secretarial toil.

Back copies of exams pose other problems. Reading the questions on exams that have been given by a certain teacher over a period of years can be of enormous value. How that teacher thinks, how he expects students to think, and what he considers to be worthy of careful study can all be gleaned from a careful reading of exam questions. Note that I said a reading of the *questions*. The danger in the use of back exams is the temptation to concentrate on, or even memorize, the answers.

The problem with memorizing answers is the same as always: It can be done without using the thinking part of the brain. It's study without learning. Carrying a headful of answers is not the same as understanding. Using old exams just to get answers has been known to backfire as well. Most teachers know that their old exams are making the rounds. Now and then one of them will lay a trap for the unwary. They will use a familiar-looking question, but rewritten to change its intent dramatically, and so the thrust of an acceptable answer.

The best strategy for using old exams is to study the questions. They tell you a lot about both the subject and the person teaching it. You will learn a great deal by working out, or digging out, good answers on your own. You learn nothing by storing someone else's answers in short-term memory.

Choices and Consequences

A very young child who upsets a cup and spills hot coffee on himself will scream in rage and pain, but will not understand that he brought the agony on himself. Coming to recognize cause and effect is a big step in a child's development. Not until years later will he routinely anticipate the effects of his actions. Only the truly mature come finally to accept the responsibility for the consequences of their actions. Choices also have consequences, and making a choice means accepting responsibility for whatever happens as a result of that choice. New college students who have worked for some years, or who have started or reared a family before entering college, do better generally, all else being equal, than their 19-year-old counterparts. One reason is the practice they've had in anticipating and accepting responsibility for the consequences of their actions. Most people, for example, have some source of money that is fairly constant. Income does not, except in the case of government, simply increase in response to spending habits. Money spent on golf clubs or a stereo is no longer available for groceries or textbooks. So it is with most choices. Choosing one thing means not choosing another. Making a choice means living with one set of consequences rather than another. Do I do the assignment or hang out? Which set of consequences do I want to live with?

A fresh look at responsibility should be part of your strategy for success. College can be unforgiving, as can some college teachers. Those who have been around a while have heard all the excuses, most of which attempt to shift responsibility to some thing or some other person. Some teachers (not all) will give even well-worn stories the benefit of the doubt and allow postponements, but that puts the student back at Square One, facing the same choices a second time. Doing the easy or comfortable thing whenever faced with a choice is a hard habit to break. Partying at the end of a semester instead of reviewing for finals can have disastrous consequences. Shifting blame to your roommate will change nothing.

College will allow you to make bad choices—one of the unadvertised aspects of freedom. Colleges are not good at protecting people from themselves. Freedom to choose means freedom to make bad choices, and all choices have consequences. One possible consequence of choosing freely is that you might not graduate in four years, or at all. A college is very liberal about dropping courses, for example. Freshmen who find themselves in a deep hole at midterm are quite relieved to learn that they can drop a science or language course or whatever is causing the most trouble. It's easy and there appear to be no consequences. No one calls your mother or sends a stern letter. But there *are* consequences. They may not show up for a couple years, but they are unavoidable. If you need five courses per semester to graduate in 4 years, what happens if during one semester you have taken only four courses? Unless you take a summer course or an overload, you can't graduate in 4 years. Suppose you need a C average to graduate and after 4 years you have a C-minus? Same result: no degree. Suppose the college requires three courses in science and you take only two. Again, you need a summer session before the degree is awarded. Admittedly, these are hard lessons, but it's better to learn them from a book than from the still harder school of experience.

One very useful thing you can do for yourself is to lay out a tentative, or make-believe, schedule for all eight semesters of college for a hypothetical student. The idea here is not to plan your own life in detail—you're likely to change your mind about a great many things in 4 years. The point is to have on paper one possible sequence of courses that would guarantee graduation on schedule. Compare your make-believe schedule of courses with the requirements of your department and the college to see that you've accounted for all of them. Your advisor can help with this, but, again, rely more on official documents such as the catalog or departmental requirement sheets. If there is a fine arts requirement, did you include that somewhere? Language? Science? Literature? Social sciences? Upper-division courses (these usually have higher numbers)? Total number of credits to graduate? Later you can make a "skeleton" schedule for yourself, listing requirements but leaving blanks for courses you will choose as you progress.

Some students are shocked to learn that the *college* does not keep track of these matters for them and see to it that courses meeting all the requirements are scheduled as needed. Help can be had for the asking, but responsibility for meeting all the requirements lies ultimately with the student. You can see the importance of getting connected with an advisor early on. Strategy and planning are what advisors are good at. Of course, neither they nor anyone else can undo what's already been done, or make happen what should have happened two years ago. The only way to escape unpleasant consequences is to avoid unwise choices. Doing so will depend on having a good attitude and good information. Information is always available, but attitude is yours alone, as is the responsibility for your choices. Maturity is never having to say "Someone should have stopped me."

nine

Exams

Student Voices

HOW COULD I GET A D? I STUDIED 18 STRAIGHT HOURS
FOR THAT FINAL!

—TONY

ome new college students are surprised to learn that in some courses there are no exams. Courses without exams are usually upper-division offerings in literature, poetry, the fine arts, and a few other areas where evaluation is subjective. The assumption in these cases is that the assigned work or performance, if well done, is in itself an indicator that you have learned what is required. Most of your courses, however, will have exams.

In some courses, instructors use nothing but exams to evaluate your performance and determine a grade. This fact has led to the widespread notion that exams are what college is all about. If the earlier chapters of this book have been persuasive, you will agree that this is not the case. Even so, knowing that your evaluation, and therefore your grade, will be determined solely by what you can do in two or three one-hour periods (or, in some cases, on a final exam only) can cause pressure and anxiety. When it does, we can have another case of positive feedback, this time of a type more commonly called a *vicious circle*. When the output of a positive feedback system is good, things simply get better. When the output is undesirable, feedback makes things still worse. In this case, anxiety detracts from your performance on an exam and therefore on your evaluation. Bad evaluations are upsetting and contribute to increased anxiety, and the vicious circle has begun to spin.

But vicious circles can be broken by eliminating one of the two factors: in the present case, by reducing the anxiety or improving performance. A circle, by definition, has no starting place, so it's impossible to know where it began. But when you attempt to break the circle, you must choose a place to start. Many pages of advice have been written on how to attack test anxiety. I will not repeat any of that here because I think the better place to attack is performance. Anxiety is incompatible with the knowledge that you have done well on exams and the conviction that you can, and probably will, do well again. Naturally, as with musicians about to perform, there is likely to be a little last-minute nervousness—you are about to be exposed to critical evaluation—but both the practiced pianist and the prepared student know that disaster is not about to strike, and their nervousness disappears the instant they get down to it. Nervousness is natural, even healthy; it's the way our systems prepare for a challenge. Anxiety, on the other hand, is distracting, debilitating, and increases the probability of disaster.

Imagine that you have a high-paying job that you love, and the supervisor calls you in to say that the company is about to "downsize." You will be interviewed in one week. The interview will consist primarily of questions put to you, and your answers will determine whether you are kept on or terminated. The supervisor will not tell you anything about the questions you will be asked except that they will be challenging.

If anyone set out to create intense anxiety, they could do no better than set up the situation I've just described. This scenario has that combination of elements guaranteed to induce stress: a possible catastrophe looming, helplessness in the face of it, and a lot of time to fret over it all.

Students who experience real anxiety over exams (not just nervousness) see them, likewise, as potential disasters, which to some extent they are, and as events that are out of their hands—over which they have no control. If the vicious circle has a weak spot, it is this presumed lack of control. Stress melts away as soon as you get control of a situation. Virtually everything I will have to say about exams is aimed at gaining control of the situation.

Remembering and Understanding

Some folks seems to be blessed, in the sense that they have been provided with a superb set of neural connections. They are said to be smart, or intelligent. The question of how much of this is genetic and what part is due to early training is still much debated. What is not debatable is that the so-called smart people do not always do well on all their college exams. Nor do people who study a great deal always do well on all *their* exams. Why would this be so?

Highly intelligent students can usually follow an explanation or discussion and immediately feel comfortable with the matter at hand. They "get it" right away. Having this natural or developed talent, such students, particularly during the first year, tend not to concern themselves further with something they understand immediately. They are confident that it will come to them when needed—that is, during an exam. Some spend almost none of their unscheduled time on coursework and simply look over their notes before an exam. Should they encounter a truly challenging exam, they may find that those things they understood at one time do not, in fact, come to them when needed.

Bright people who catch on quickly and still score poorly on some exams are more common than you would expect. They run into this trouble because a well-designed and challenging exam tests both understanding and memory. Understanding requires certain talent, skill, and effort, but the ability to explain requires something else—a verbal memory of what was understood. The kind of exam that causes this problem will be described later, along with some reasons why memory often fails.

Some students, on the other hand, find that things go much too rapidly in class and try to compensate by working hard to remember everything that was said or written. They come to exams with a great number of facts in their heads, but if the exam is designed to test understanding, those facts, even when transcribed accurately, do not earn high marks. For the truly challenging exam, both understanding and memory are required, and the memory must be verbal—what is understood must be capable of being summoned up in words. The correlation between learning and grades is again obvious. True learning means understanding, remembering, and verbalizing—just the things that guarantee a good performance on exams.

Kinds of Exams

Nevertheless, everyone knows, or will quickly learn, that there are different kinds of exams. Some are, frankly, not challenging at all; others are little short of diabolical. But in addition to coming in different degrees of difficulty, they also vary in format. For the sake of simplicity, I will lump them all into two categories: those in which you select answers, and those in which you generate answers. When an exam requires you to select an answer from a list, we call it multiple-choice (MC). Somewhat less precisely, we call exams "essay exams" when there are only questions and you must generate the answers in words of your own. Answers on this kind of exam are not always essays in the true sense. Sometimes an extended definition is expected, or perhaps one or more sentences. The important distinction here is not the number of words or sentences a good answer will require, but the fact that you must generate the answer from what you have in your head and your own vocabulary.

You should understand that the difficulty of an exam is not necessarily correlated with its format. In some courses, particularly those in engineering, mathematics, and some of the sciences, a selection-type test can be quite mind-boggling. There is simply no way of knowing from memory which answer makes sense, nor will clever guessing help. Only a great deal of thinking, including application of known principles, calculations, derivations, or proofs can lead you to the correct choice. Selection exams can, on the other hand, be mere exercises in recognizing a key word here or there and eliminating the obviously silly. Similar arguments can be made to show that the so-called essay-type exam, in which you must supply the entire answer, can be either trivial or very difficult. The challenge an exam presents does not correlate with the type of exam or even the field of study; everything depends on the teacher who makes up the exam.

Preparing

Ideally, there would be no such thing as preparing for an exam, in the sense of doing anything beyond what you would routinely do to learn the subject matter. Anyone who learned new material in reasonable chunks by reading, making and filling in notes, and writing paraphrases (or solving all the problems in cases where that is the learning process) would always be ready for an exam—with one exception. For those MC exams that test only your ability to retain an incredible number of isolated small facts, there is nothing to do but sit down and stuff your head. You may wonder, as I do, what the purpose of such exams is, but if that is what's required, then that's what you do. For this kind of exam, you will find study techniques in many books and pamphlets on improving memory, and there is no need to repeat them here. In this one case only is it helpful to compress your study into a short period just before the exam, because these facts will begin trickling out of your head almost as fast as you put them in.

Of serious concern here are the times when you study as described above—cramming, pulling "all-nighters" and the like—and still do miserably on exams. What you have encountered in these cases is a teacher who expects more than recall and recognition learning. You have encountered the *challenging exam*.

Serious exams, like serious learning, are matters of language. This is true in mathematics and science as well; you just encounter and use a different set of symbols. Most of what I have said about learning has involved language in some way, and the truly challenging exam is simply an extension of the process of learning. The best way to approach an exam is to think of it as a performance. If you set out in your German class to actually learn German (and not just "take" it), then you will have been reading German, writing German, and building a vocabulary all along. The exam will be just a time to show what you know: a performance in language.

This way of seeing things might, again, be thought heroic and not something to be aspired to by mere mortals. In fact, a surprising and gratifying number of students achieve this level of learning, and there is no reason what-soever that you should not be one of them. A few students have even let slip the fact that they enjoy exams—one young woman found them "fun!"

I think the word *fun* was misused in that case, but I understand com-pletely her intent. I have repeatedly used the analogy of the musician who learns and practices until the music is stuck in his head and hands. The learn-ing and practice in these cases is absolutely gratifying and satisfying—it cannot be dreary toil or it would not get done. Nevertheless, every musician or athlete secretly wants to perform, and to perform well. *Bravo* and *brava* are the sweet-est words in the world to performers. For the student, the intellectual equiva-lent is an A on a paper or 95 percent on an exam.

Understandably, new students might believe that exams are given only be-cause the teacher needs some way to generate a grade for each student. That kind of thinking, however, turns the whole process on its head. Grades are not at all necessary. Most college teachers would prefer that there be no course grades. We have them because students insist on it. Were teachers to simply teach and let the amount of learning be determined by the students' desire, there would soon be rebellion. Parents and employers would find that a fair percentage of graduates had not taken advantage of the opportunities given them and had emerged from college older but no wiser. Students would com-plain that there should be some way of knowing whether or not they were re-ally learning the subject matter. Exams allow students to find out that they are, or are not, doing the right things to learn; exams would be necessary even if there were no grades.

Believing that exams are chances to perform, and not sadistic inventions to ruin your life, will very much influence your attitude and therefore your ap-proach to them. You will see exams (if they are not trivial) as extensions of what you are already doing. If you are learning as you go, participating in classroom discussions, working in study groups, reading, making notes, solv-ing problems, paraphrasing, and using assignments as intended, the exam is not going to present you with much that is new or surprising. If, on the other hand, you study only in order to pass an exam, it is almost inevitable that you will not start until the exam appears on the horizon and then find yourself faced with a huge amount of unfamiliar material to be "learned" in a short time. Learning, which is best done leisurely, in a stress-free environment, and is normally enjoyable, becomes grinding toil when attempted under great pres-sure. It isn't learning at all; more like hardening yourself for a terrible ordeal.

It follows, then, that students can put themselves in a position where no advice is possible. When seen only as obstacles to good grades, exams can only be unpleasant, and postponing preparation becomes the natural thing to do. But challenging exams cannot be prepared for by cramming, and students who try it put themselves in an impossible situation. You can cram for those massive 150-question tests where to answer you make a dark dot with a No. 2 pencil, but if you are given a blue book and questions that start out, "What were the political conditions that led to . . ." or "How is it that all the cells of the body . . ." or "Compare Alexis de Tocqueville's *Democracy in America* with . . . ," then your cramming will have been in vain. The knowledge required to answer questions of this sort has to be gotten slowly, in small bits, reviewed periodically, and talked about—it must have become a part of you.

The best preparation for a difficult exam was exemplified by a young man taking calculus. For one week before the exam, he devoted a half hour each night to reworking sample problems of all the types that had been on the assignments (which, of course, he had been doing faithfully). The day of the exam, which was at 4:00 P.M., he ate lunch, took a two-hour nap, had a refreshing shower, took the exam, and blew it away.

If an exam requires serious learning—beyond recall and recognition—the learning must be done as described throughout the earlier chapters of this book, not attempted in one or two nights. Even so, as exam time approaches, everyone begins to feel some nervousness and tension, and a real need to do a little something extra. Preparation for challenging exams, then, comes in two parts: remote preparation and immediate preparation. The better students never neglect either. Remote preparation is simply learning as I have described it. We turn now to immediate preparation, always bearing in mind that immediate preparation is not a substitute for learning.

Immediate Preparation

Assume you've done it all just right. You have learned what was intended in every assignment, read the suggested books, made detailed and paraphrased notes, talked about the subject in study groups, and used the expert—the teacher—to clear up uncertainties and check your version of things. What do you do now, when the exam is coming up? Even the most learned student, the one who has done everything we might call remote preparation, needs to get warmed up for the actual performance. What constitutes a warmup will vary with the content material. In the humanities and social sciences (assuming always that the exam is not trivial), the first thing to do is make an educated guess at the topics likely to show up. Often a teacher will tell you in a general way what the topics will be. Obviously, these should be reviewed, but review does not mean paging though the notebook and staring for several minutes at each page.

Review for a written exam has two important aspects. First, we must remember that the "I know it but I can't say it" problem is always ready to strike us dumb. What has been read, digested, and understood may still elude us when the pencil is in the hand and an empty sheet of paper stares blankly back at us. Warmup, in this case, means writing. I know of no better way to do the immediate preparation for an exam than to make up sample questions and write answers to them. And the writing is essential. You really don't know that you can write an answer to a question until you try it. This exercise is beneficial even if the questions you make up don't appear on the actual exam. When you first attempt to write on any topic in the subject area, names, vocabulary, and facts that you thought you would remember tend to slip away, so you will need to refresh your memory. This final checking, rechecking, and writing solidifies things in the mind.

Rereading is the second part of review in the less technical fields. Rereading, if it is really that, can be done quite rapidly. I warned earlier that you could not really learn sixty pages of challenging material in one night. That remains true, but if you have actually already learned it once and this is truly review, it all comes back quickly, and you can read profitably many pages in a short time. What you are doing is running one more time through familiar neural pathways in the brain. The assumption here is that you already understand; the immediate review is to help you remember.

In fields like chemistry and math, writing is equally essential in the immediate review. If the last time you balanced an oxidation/reduction equation was 30 days ago, those neural pathways definitely need to be reinforced. Get the pencil and paper and do it one more time. It will go fast and will be easy; if it isn't, you have definitely discovered something you thought you would remember but don't.

Reviewing without pencil and paper is not very effective. Many new college students review for exams by doing something they call "going through their notes." They stare intently at each page in succession, and when they get to the end, they start over and do it all again. This is repeated over and over, right up until the instant the exam is put in their hands. This behavior is comforting, but not very useful. Those students are simply becoming familiar with their notebooks. The more times they see something, the more convinced they become that they know it.

A young woman reviewing for a biology exam had looked a dozen or more times at the page with her labeled drawing of the digestive system. The word *pancreas* was there, a word familiar to her from grade school. She would have recognized it anywhere. The actual exam question was "What is the pancreas and what does it do for you?" That young woman was unable to write anything specific about the pancreas. *Pancreas* was a familiar symbol, but one that had no real meaning for her. If, during her review, she had tried to write a small essay on what the pancreas does, she would have discovered before it was too late that she had never really learned anything about the pancreas. Reviewing must be more than recognizing.

I should remind you one last time that the kind of preparation I have been describing only works if it is really review. You cannot, in a few hours, learn for the first time all the chemistry that might be covered in a month of classes.

Lewis Thomas wrote a provocative essay called "The Scrambler in the Mind," in which he proposes the whimsical theory that the brain has a mechanism for protecting itself from overload. He describes his own experience of trying to learn quantum mechanics from an expert in one afternoon. His tutor was an excellent teacher and things were going remarkably well. Dr. Thomas thought that finally, in his maturity, he would learn quantum mechanics. He found himself understanding everything that was said. But at a certain point, trying to relate new material to what had come before became a surprising strain. As he struggled to put it all together, a remarkable thing happened. He lost it all! Everything he had heard from the beginning became a hopeless jumble. He understood nothing.

It's an interesting story. Dr. Thomas may have exaggerated a tiny bit in the telling, but the point of the story is quite valid. The brain is probably the most complex structure evolution has yet produced, and capable of far more than any of us ever demands of it, but it does have limitations. The brain likes things to come in reasonable-sized chunks. Try cramming it with too much in too short a period and it rebels, or, if Lewis Thomas is correct, it protects itself by garbling everything—almost as if it had a "delete/reset" button. I suspect something of this sort happens to students who study all night and then find that their minds go blank during the exam.

Timing

You will have noticed that many of my ideas on learning and things mental are based on the biological functioning of the brain. Few would argue with this approach. But a surprising number of new students do not treat their brain as an organ made up of cells, and having the demands and limitations of other organs. People who would laugh at the idea of starting to get into condition for a marathon two days before the race will nevertheless start getting ready for an exam a matter of hours before it is scheduled.

The brain needs rest as surely as your other parts do. The lad who took a nap several hours before an exam was making the best possible use of his brain. Some students have the mistaken notion that if they sleep, everything they have learned will in some way dissolve. It is true that the brain seems to have a short-term processing system that is different from what is called long-term memory. We can retain word sequences—sentences—nearly verbatim for several seconds, until other parts of the brain abstract meaning and make sense of what we heard. Within minutes, the exact words we heard will indeed be gone, but if we have extracted their meaning, we will be able to paraphrase because the ideas behind the words will have gone into long-term memory.

Exam review, if it is indeed review, is not putting things into short-term memory; it is reinforcing what was put into long-term memory, bit by bit, over an extended period. So if you review in the true sense, there need be no fear that knowledge will drain out of your ear into the pillow at night. In fact, if you don't rest the brain before you call on it to perform, it may poop out in the middle of it all, or, worse yet, rebel and scramble everything.

So here is a simple idea: Always give the brain a rest before you ask it to perform at its best. "Studying" right up to the last possible instant tends to induce panic. Students who are still frantically flipping through the pages of their notebooks as the exams are being distributed do themselves no favor.

Never, never, never study all night the night before an exam! If you insist on doing this at least once, so you'll have a story to tell your grandchildren, pick an exam that you know will require only recall and recognition; don't try it for integral calculus or molecular genetics. Staying awake for 20 hours before an exam is counterproductive in the extreme. As we will see below, the actual taking of the exam can be mentally and physically exhausting. You need to be fresh and relaxed. How unwise to totally exhaust yourself just before the big performance! If you were to play in a tennis match final at 9:00 A.M., would you play tennis all night to get ready? Your brain is a physical organ. You abuse it at your own peril.

If you think of an exam as being similar to an athletic or musical performance, then you'll prepare for it the same way. You'll always be "in shape," meaning that you could do a reasonable job of it without any preparation at all. You would sharpen your skills and work with more concentration as the big day approached. But you would definitely get a good night's sleep just before, and be as refreshed and rested as possible. A brief warmup to get the juices flowing and you're ready.

Good athletes and good musicians put themselves up for public evaluation believing that they are not about to make fools of themselves. The athletes may not win that day, and the musician may not play as well as he knows he can, but there won't be a disaster. So they may feel a little nervous tension, but the assurance that they are prepared and can do well prevents the debilitating stress and anxiety that would indeed bring on a disaster.

Having such assurance, and the confidence it inspires, is the only reliable way to avoid test anxiety and the resulting vicious circle. Meditation, yoga, or tranquilizers cannot produce a good performance, and so cannot offer a long-term solution for anxiety. Only a performance that meets your own expectations can provide that self-assurance required to prevent future debilitating stress. And only serious learning can guarantee a good performance.

During the Exam

From time to time I hear a freshman enter the examination room muttering, "I've done all I can, it's out of my hands now," or something similar. Such students are burdened by a terribly incorrect belief, which has somehow become "common knowledge" and detracts seriously from good performance on exams. It's as if the preparation consisted of meticulously filling a vessel and the exam were nothing but spilling it all out. But clearly, the point of the exam is to demonstrate understanding, and that is not something that can be done without effort. Convincing someone else that you are knowledgeable about a subject is demanding work. For the limited purpose of *demonstrating* knowledge, what you do during the exam is more important than how hard you worked getting ready.

So what's wrong with the "It's out of my hands" attitude? First of all, it embodies one of the elements of anxiety. Remember that anxiety comes when there is the potential for disaster *and* you believe that there's nothing you can do—that it's out of your hands. Second, it is totally inconsistent with the attitude that the exam is performance. No athlete or musician would ever suggest that practice takes care of everything and that the performance is out of his hands.

In the case of a challenging exam, be prepared to focus the mind and concentrate with still more intensity than you did during the learning and the preparing. Taking an exam is harder work than getting ready for it. That's why I insisted that it's necessary to be rested and alert. That word *challenging* does not mean that the exam questions will be about obscure items, or require absolutely accurate recall of a lot of information; *challenging* means that the exam is one that will require the *use* of all your skills of reasoning, recall, and expression. The emphasis is on use. Successful test takers do not believe that the exam is a time to unload information, but more a chance to *use* everything they have ever learned to figure out answers to new problems. Using information to solve new problems is a matter of thinking. It's hard work, and it can't be done by a tired brain.

Using information rather than unloading it is the key to good performance. In fact, it is this demand that information be used and not just reported that causes so many new students to characterize college exams as tricky or unfair. Being asked to answer a question you've never seen before, or to solve a novel problem, can be a shock if you've never faced that kind of challenge before.

Still, this aspect of the challenging exam is one of the things that makes the college experience truly practical. Life after schooling is a matter of coping. Relationships with other people, finances, children, and work all require solving novel problems. Few of life's significant concerns are settled by knowing the answer to a specific question you encountered as a freshman. Getting along without trauma, however, may very well depend on being able to analyze a pressing problem and figure out a course of action. And that, in turn, will depend on knowing how things work and how people have approached similar problems in the past—what worked and what didn't. Exams that make just these kinds of demands are absolutely realistic. They give the lie to the preposterous claim that the "real world" lies only outside formal learning.

Our goal, then, must be to ensure that you will not, after serious learning and proper preparation, do all the wrong things while actually taking the exam.

Expect the Unexpected

The exam that does not have some surprises cannot be considered challenging. It may be long and tiresome, and may put demands on your short-term memory, but if you can do it without turning on the thinking part of the brain, then it is simply an exercise in recall. A good exam is like a hockey game: You have to have all the skills and know all the plays, but the real challenge is to be able to react to the unexpected—to make a play you've never done before because the situation demands it. The young woman who thought exams were fun reveled in the novel and the unexpected on exams. Here, at last, was a chance to use what she knew—to discover, through reasoning and application, something she hadn't known before.

Learning During the Exam

There are certainly many new college students who would be quite puzzled at the suggestion that they try to learn *while* taking an exam. The "accepted wisdom" is that before the exam you learn, and during the exam you unload what you have learned. That may be accepted, but it isn't wisdom. The time to learn during an exam is when you encounter the unexpected, and, as I have mentioned, in good courses with challenging exams, that might be fairly frequently. Consider the examples given below.

Some teachers are fond of the hypothetical question. *Hypothetical* is not a bad word. It does not mean false or silly. What the hypothetical question does is set up unreal conditions in order to test your ability to apply known principles and rules to a novel or unusual situation (like life again). Hypothetical questions start most often with *If*, or *Assuming*. The intent is to set up a situation that you have never encountered and to see whether you would know what to do if you really did encounter it. A physics question, designed to test your skills with gravitation problems, might start out, "If the moon were made of blue cheese," and go on to tell you the density and other details about blue cheese. Finally, it might ask you some question about tide levels or the length of the lunar month. The unimaginative student who has read the chapter on the moon will proceed to "correct" the question and give the real composition of the moon and its real density to four significant figures. The curious student *accepts* the hypothetical part of the question as *true for the moment*, starts to wonder, "How would the tides be affected if the mass of the moon changed?", and immediately becomes absorbed in figuring out this puzzle.

Question 3 on a biology exam might ask, "Is *all* arterial blood more highly oxygenated than venous blood?" The thinking student, remembering that she had in fact always thought that arterial blood was bright red and therefore oxygenated, wonders what the point of this question really is, and begins a quick but careful review of circulation. There will be a sudden awareness that, indeed, there are arteries that carry deoxygenated blood. She will then proceed to describe the situation in which that condition exists.

A math question might be: "Assume a driver makes a lap around the Indianapolis Speedway's two-and-a-half-mile track at an average speed of 160 miles per hour and then makes a second lap at 200 miles per hour. What is the driver's average speed for the two laps?" The student who expects the unexpected, and is used to learning new things during an exam, will do a complete analysis of the conditions, use her understanding of *average* and *rate,* and discover that *the answer is not 180 miles per hour.*

Further Pitfalls

The examples above all assume a well-prepared test taker, but also a curious one. Seeing the exam as an ordeal to be got through, and the quicker the better, is not conducive to the type of wondering and figuring out that those examples required. Being prepared to do some strenuous thinking and some learning during the exam will enable you to avoid another pitfall that catches the unwary. I'm thinking of the typical question that asks something unusual about a common and well-known topic. Imagine a question that started, "What would Thomas Hobbes have thought about our current situation regarding . . ." Such a question is, again, hypothetical, because Hobbes is long dead and cannot have any thoughts about our current situation. The purpose of the question is to discover what you know: first, about Hobbes; second, about current affairs; finally, about the applicability of historical thought to contemporary problems. The danger here is that of fastening on some key word and writing a set piece that you have learned in advance. Someone who had studied the chapter on Hobbes, and had committed to memory a summary of his philosophy, will be tempted to simply download that information onto paper. This practice produces a phenomenon that puzzles and infuriates a number of new students: a paragraph consisting of accurate information that does not answer the question, and therefore receives a low grade. Teachers who give challenging exams find themselves writing in the margins, "Read the question." They mean this quite literally. The student has learned a chunk of something not with the intention of *using* that information, but only of having it. The student expectation is that stored information is to be replayed on an exam. But the teacher who gives a challenging exam expects the application and use of information, not merely its storage and unloading. "Read the question" means "Dig out the intent." When a question starts with *If* or *How* or

Why, or includes instructive words such as *related to,* or *in comparison with,* or *under conditions of,* that question must be read with more than common care so that its intent is thoroughly understood. Reading a question only to find the topic can lead to answers that are irrelevant; the point of reading the question is to find out what it is you are being asked to do. Always do what the question instructs you to do.

The Clock as Friend

Most exams are timed, and this in itself puts the student in the kind of double bind I spoke of in Chapter 7, "Between Classes"—having both a set amount of work to do and a specific period of time in which it must be done. You simply have to accept that, and learn a trick or two to prevent the stress that such a condition usually generates. On an exam for which you must write answers or solve problems, and for which you are prepared, you should find a few questions that you recognize, maybe even one or two that you anticipated and practiced on during preparation. There are few things in the world more calming than spotting an "old friend" on an exam. Do these first and as quickly as is consistent with a complete and correct answer. Then check the clock and tell yourself, "Two questions done and still 30 minutes left." This is pure psychological trickery, but we need all the help we can get. If you check the clock only to find out how little time is left, it will always be too little.

When you are stuck—and it will happen a lot—staring into space or looking blankly at the page is not a good way to think. Use the pencil. Sometimes a question that at first looked totally unfamiliar will turn out to be a well-known idea or process that is being applied to a novel situation. Seeing the connection might be a matter of luck, but you raise your odds by pushing the pencil while you are thinking. Write definitions, list the things you know about the key elements of the question, scribble out some "what-if" trial balloons. Writing anything relevant makes the brain work. If it is not working, it will begin feeling sorry for itself and concentrating on how rapidly the time is passing.

Use Everything You Have Ever Learned

When something is really true, not just hypothetically true, it is true for all time and in all situations. That means you can use what you know from history to support an answer in economics. It means algebra is always good and might help, or even be essential, in the middle of a chemistry problem. The rules of chemistry apply in all cases to life and may be needed to answer questions in biology. Needless to say, you must never dispense with the rules of good writing; they apply everywhere. If you are taking a sociology exam, you cannot put yourself in a sociology box and ignore the facts of biology, history, and psychology and the rules of mathematics. Everything that is true can be used on any exam.

However, that bit of liberating news must be qualified to prevent another common error on exams. Robert Fulghum wrote a book entitled *All I Really Need to Know I Learned in Kindergarten.* He might have written another, entitled *All I Really Need to Know for College I Learned in the Sixth Grade.* An amazing amount of stuff from grade school sticks in our heads. Some of it is still true, some was true then but isn't now, some of it was misunderstood, and some was wrong. But, right, wrong, or irrelevant, it sticks in our heads and springs up at the proper cue. These scraps of information, or misinformation, can do mischief on a college exam. Dispatching a subtle and complicated college exam question with a tidbit remembered from grade school is not a good idea. One young man did himself a grave disservice by basing his answer to a question on the "fact" that plants do not contain proteins. That plants do not have proteins is not a fact at all; indeed, it is blatantly false. But he had learned years ago in a health class that plants were sources of vitamins and minerals, and that meat, fish, and eggs were sources of protein. This partial truth, intended to advise the very young on eating habits, had through all the intervening years prevented him from assimilating more complete and useful information about the nature of living things. So do use whatever is true during an exam, but be quite sure that it is true.

Chance Favors the Prepared Mind

Finally, there is an element of luck on most exams. Sometimes you will guess just right as to what ideas, processes, or principles the exam will stress and you will have prepared by writing small essays on these. At such times, life is sweet. But luck is a minor element at best. No one is consistently lucky or unlucky on exams.

If you have learned well all along, practiced talking about the subject in study groups, written practice essays, rested well before the exam, and gone in expecting the unexpected—ready to work hard and heat up your brain for an hour, and prepared to use everything you know to be true—you'll be amazed at how lucky you are.

ten

Autonomy

For of all sad words of tongue or pen,
The saddest are these: "It might have been!"
— *John Greenleaf Whittier*

Student Voices

I GOT Ds MY FIRST SEMESTER. THIS YEAR I'M ON THE
DEAN'S LIST. I CAN'T BELIEVE I'M SAYING IT, BUT I REALLY
LOVE SCHOOL.

—DANNY

 missed chance is truly sad when the opportunity will never come again. You might miss a weekend at the beach, but there will be others. And the ski slopes will fill up with snow for years to come. Some opportunities, however, like the perfect job, come only once or twice in a lifetime. College is such an opportunity, and it is indeed sad when it is missed. It is true that a few do return to college a second time to take advantage of what they missed the first, but it is rare.

Someone whose lifestyle or interests have changed considerably since college might look back and wonder whether he should have gone to a different kind of college or majored in a different area. It is possible, however, that the missed opportunity was not that of choosing the right school or major, but one of the greatest opportunities any college has to offer—the chance to achieve autonomy.

I use the word *autonomy* here not so much in the political sense of self-governing, but more in the biological sense of independent and free-standing. Because we are a social species, no one is ever completely independent—absolute autonomy is not possible. But the greater your ability to act independently, the better your chances of taking advantage of the new opportunities the future holds. To regain an opportunity that is really lost, you would have to turn back the clock. An opportunity that requires not turning the clock back, but having certain knowledge, information, or skill, is seldom closed to anyone who acquired the learning habit in college. The autonomous graduate will not need to turn back the clock—to return to college—in order to learn what is needed to take advantage of new opportunities. The autonomous graduate no longer needs the college.

As used here, *autonomy* can be simply defined. It is the ability to learn without a teacher. That is what is meant by equating autonomy with independence. *Independence* has come to suggest a certain undisciplined bullheadedness—even unruliness. I use the word here in its earlier sense of not having to depend on someone else. *Independent,* then, will mean only that one is generally capable of doing for oneself, particularly when it comes to knowing what to think.

Being able to arrive at a position through independent analysis pays a number of unexpected dividends. One's major, for example, loses the confining or restrictive character often associated with it. You are also far less likely to be taken in by fast talkers.

Our earlier characterization of education—as relieving you of the burden of having to believe everything you are told—has the notion of autonomy written into it. The intent was not to imply that autonomy makes you incapable of error, or that any thought or belief is as good as any other. Being autonomous means, rather, that you will be able to uncover truth without benefit of teachers and classrooms. The autonomous learner will discover and use sources other than a single authority. The education that leads to autonomy will include, right from the beginning, doing those things that wean a student from dependence on teachers. Clearly students who consider education to be no more than holding the words of teachers in their heads cannot become independent. You will recall that the educated person will be able to tell when a man is talking rot. Now, if your training consists precisely in believing everything you are told, the idea of examining the content of what you hear or read will remain forever foreign to you.

These ideas make the relation of teacher to student somewhat slippery. What is the role of the teacher on this path toward autonomy? How does a student learn from teachers, all the while trying to become independent of them? In the first place, teachers who have their students' best interests at heart *want* to make themselves dispensable. Students should not see college as a filling station, and teachers should not see their job as that of filling students' heads. Although teachers do dispense facts in abundance, the most valuable thing they do for their students is to get them to learn on their own—on their own time and on their own initiative. New teachers often get advice from their more senior colleagues in the form of a very old proverb: Give a hungry man a fish and he will be hungry again tomorrow. Teach him to catch fish and he will never be hungry again.

Why Now?

ndependent thinking and autonomy are serious and difficult ideas. Why think about such things here, at the beginning? It's because independent learning is a developed skill. You learn to do it only by doing it. Your very first writing assignment could be your first halting step on a journey toward independent learning and autonomy. Clear thinking and the precise use of language are not things that just happen. Start now. Every Olympic gymnast was once a clumsy little kid. Slow, steady progress is the key to a well-developed mind as well as body.

The ability to learn independently is not a guaranteed outcome of being awarded a degree. Nor can it be learned by taking a course in critical thinking. As do all skills, independent learning becomes habitual only through repetition over time. Even in technical fields—perhaps especially in technical fields—the things learned are not so important as the process of learning them. Some successful engineers have said that 95 percent of what they use in their career was learned after they left college. Such a state of affairs is certainly not consistent with the idea that you go to college to learn those things you will need to know to earn a living for the rest of your life. But it is consistent with our recurring theme, that college provides only opportunity, and the education you leave with will be the one you have given yourself. What you want to take away from college is an inclination toward continued learning and the skill and experience to do it.

The engineers who learn most of what they need to know on their own are certainly not unique examples. Everyday living, if it is not to be continually frustrating, requires that very ability to learn what you need to know. You have probably heard that there are millions of VCRs sitting in American homes, blinking 12:00, because their owners can't program them. This has often been blamed on malicious engineers who delight in making things too complex for mere mortals. There may be an element of truth in that, but our having come to expect that the complex can always be made easy is probably the more significant factor. Life is full of messy things that need our attention; taxes, insurance, leases, licenses, lawyers, and sump pumps, to name a few. There are many things that are inherently complex, but must still be attended to. Which means you must continue to learn if you do not wish to remain dependent on others every time something new comes along.

A person who discovers and becomes skilled in the process of learning might be compared to a child who learns to walk. Once children get walking into their systems, they will walk everywhere. After a relatively short time, walking is automatic—unpremeditated. Your goal in college should be to make learning equally automatic. You will simply do it when you need to, as naturally as walking to the refrigerator.

And what is it you will actually be doing? Rarely will it involve more than making an accurate connection between cause and effect and extracting the intended meaning from the spoken or written word—or, in some cases, recognizing that there is no meaning. A life spent figuring things out has much to be said for it.

What Do I Do Now?

If independent learning and the autonomy it brings are acquired skills, it follows that your first attempts might feel strange. But you have to start somewhere, and useful and satisfying results can be had right from the beginning. I believe the first step, small but immensely important, occurs when a student wonders, "How do they know that?" How different from "Tell me what I need to know." "How do you know that?" sets the stage for autonomy. The student who works his way back to first principles, firsthand accounts, or experimental results, no matter how simple the problem, is doing independent learning. That student, on the other hand, who asks only for "the answers" will stay dependent on someone to provide answers, possibly for the rest of his life.

Some students seem to be "naturals" at independent learning. Even as children they had to get to the bottom of things. What makes a clock work? How can you make a doll's dress from just cloth and thread? Where does bread come from? How do the baby chicks get inside the eggs? These childish questions demonstrate the natural curiosity of the human mind. The pursuit of answers to some of these seemingly simple questions might turn into a career that will occupy a lifetime. The new college student needs to rediscover the child's sense of wonder as to how or why things are the way they are. Those who never lost the curiosity to get to the bottom of things, and use college as a place to simply indulge that curiosity, will be the "naturals."

"What do I do now?" The first steps toward autonomy are simply those things suggested in earlier chapters for learning in general. Going to sources—books, works of art, musical scores, the laboratory, or original research—with a question in mind, a need to know, is simply practice for the day when there will be some serious thing you need to know and no teacher down the hall. Paraphrasing what you read this year will prepare you for your future reading of whatever it might be that is suddenly important to you, even if it is just the instruction manual for your VCR.

Commencement

The ceremony at which degrees are awarded is called *commencement*. The common meanings of commencement all have to do with beginning. Students who believe that graduation means the end of learning will wonder why the awarding of the diploma is called the beginning. What is it that is beginning?

What is about to begin is autonomy—not in the sense of making our own rules or disregarding authority, but rather in the sense of continuing to progress after having lost a great deal of our support system. For some graduates who have been in school continually since the age of five, commencement can come as a shock. A world without teachers, schedules, and assigned tasks can be unsettling if you have not been preparing for it. At commencement, responsibilities increase just as abruptly as the support system falls away. The training wheels are off.

For those who have used the college experience as it was intended, commencement triggers some melancholy, but not anxiety. The well-prepared graduate will have been growing less dependent on teachers and the system all along. The key word here is *growing*. As we have seen, independent learning can be compared in one way to physical strength. The world cannot be divided into those who "have strength" and those who do not. We all have strength, but to different degrees. How strong anyone eventually becomes is simply a matter of how they use their muscles. You can no more become suddenly autonomous than you can become suddenly strong. We become autonomous the same way we grow strong—little by little, over a period of time. So if graduation day should not produce anxiety, neither should it evoke hysterical jubilation. You will not in any way be changed by having a diploma placed in your hand. The changes that count have all happened in the preceding four or so years.

The Future

Dwelling on an uncertain future can be unnerving. Most of us felt uneasy at about six or seven years of age when well-meaning adults began asking us what we would become when we grew up. We didn't know then and some of us still aren't sure. But it was (and is) comforting to have an answer ready. Later, the first question people ask after being introduced is "What do you do?" It's as if we can be authenticated only through our work or profession. Similarly, "What's your major?" is the universal campus question. At times it may seem that anything is better than not having an answer. Having a major, like having a profession, seems to bestow an identity. Understandably, then, students are often uneasy until they are into a major. Unfortunately, too many students, once they have chosen a major, see it as a kind of lifelong commitment—the final decision on "what to be when I grow up."

It's the professional colleges, such as engineering, business, nursing, and hotel management, that have introduced this way of thinking. Professional schools use up so much time training students in the specifics of their profession that the graduate cannot imagine life outside that profession. What is the point of a degree in nursing if one does not then enter the nursing profession? In the arts and sciences, connecting one's life with the major is far less rigorous. The biology major need not become a biologist, nor the psychology major a psychologist. Ideally (although this is certainly not always the case), the major represents an area of concentrated study chosen because the student finds it interesting. In some majors, students need take only one third of their courses in the prescribed discipline. Such arrangements, admirable in my opinion, leave a lot of room for experimenting and learning in some depth about a number of different things. The major is not a security blanket. To trust that it represents a career, or a guarantee of employment, is to abandon your autonomy from the beginning.

The obvious truth is that none of us knows in any detail what's ahead. There are no recession-proof professions and certainly no assurances that when we actually do the thing we thought we wanted to do, it will live up to our expectations. It is these disappointments and surprises that give rise to the numerous retraining programs intended to compensate for what is essentially a chaotic state of affairs. Although the popularizers of the word *retraining* did not intend it, the word has dehumanizing overtones. *Training* always conjures up for me a vision of seals becoming skilled in balancing beach balls on their noses. You should not be trained in this sense. Ideally, the skills you acquire in college are precisely those that make retraining unnecessary; these are, of course, the habits of mind that foster independent and ongoing learning. The well-educated college graduate sees change, even dramatic change, as challenging but not frightening, and certainly not debilitating. Change simply means learning some new things. That is precisely what the autonomous graduate will be good at.

Some Illusions

To fail to become autonomous is to be forever hampered by careless, lazy, and uncritical thinking. Careless thinkers are taken in by the unscrupulous because their first impulse is to believe rather than to analyze. They chase illusions. Consider here several attractive illusions that independent thinkers learn to avoid. The first is the notion that a complex problem can be made simple by asking a simple question. Students of history who want to know why a certain war got started and who research that question in some detail will find that the simple question "Why did this war start?" masks a cauldron of complex and interacting forces, no one of which can be tagged as the cause. If we never get beyond the stage of listing the three reasons for this or the four effects of that, real situations will overwhelm us with their complexity. It is an illusion, albeit a comforting one, to believe that intrinsically complex matters can be simplified by asking simple questions.

A second and powerful illusion is that all things, including people, can be put into categories, and the categories have the power to explain. Having boxes to put things and people into is, again, comforting but simplistic. The practice is characteristic of lazy thinking. As a substitute for learning about something or someone, the lazy mind sets up boxes: a box for good things, a box for bad things, a box for conservatives, a box for liberals, one for immigrants, one for Catholics, one for homosexuals, and so on. Putting things in boxes is easier than learning about them.

How often, after a radioactive leak, for example, will the reporter ask a "box" question: "Is there any danger to residents?" This is a simple-minded question that cannot have an answer. It is a "box" question because it categorizes all substances as either safe or unsafe, dangerous or not dangerous. In reality, danger and safety come in all levels or degrees. The autonomous person is not swayed by simple-minded questions that ignore this truth. He will eventually come to realize that there is no *absolute safety,* and be prepared to evaluate the level of danger in any situation. Autonomy means throwing away the boxes and learning about the thing in question.

You may get a start on this careful kind of thinking early on, in the form of requirements. If your college insists that you learn a little math or science, it is with the hope that some day you will be able to react intelligently to statements such as "Substance X causes cancer in mice." This kind of headline serves no purpose except to alarm people. Without knowing quite a lot about how these mice were treated, you know almost nothing. What you need to learn now is something about percentages, concentrations, ratios, and how science is done if you are to make sense of newspapers and television news in the future. Without such knowledge, you put yourself at the mercy of anyone who can tell a persuasive story.

In a world of independent learners, there would be no place for hucksters and tyrants. They could not survive because their deceptions and half-truths would be examined and exposed for what they are. But only those with inquiring minds and facility with the language stop to ask the serious questions, such as "What precisely does that mean?" or "What exactly is he saying?"

Finally, when the search for true causality has become, through habit, a component of your everyday thinking, you will also have learned that attributing causality to abstractions such as "the economy" or "our society" is empty talk and points to no solution. Such comments may sound strange to you now, at the beginning of your college studies, considering the number of times *the economy* or *our society* are given as the causes of specific problems, but you have four years to determine whether or not I'm talking rot.

A Final Wish

At a certain age, the highest praise anyone can receive is to be characterized as wise. Wisdom has not come up before now, and for a reason. Effort and practice can usually guarantee learning—even that higher-level learning beyond recognition and recall—but wisdom is an elusive quality. It is not readily defined and there are no twelve-step programs that guarantee it. Still, it's possible to recognize it, and we all admire it when we find it. To paraphrase a well-known prayer, distinguishing between those things you can change through courageous action and those you must endure with calm patience is a sign of considerable wisdom. Wise people seem to know what to say and what to do, but also when to say it or do it, or when to say or do nothing. The wise person's words and actions need not always be nice, but they are always measured and appropriate. I wish I had some words that would guarantee wisdom, but it seems to settle on whomever it chooses. Even so, I suspect that, like chance, it tends to favor the prepared mind. Preparing your mind is the reason you came to college.

I cannot, then, tell you what to do to become wise. But my wish for you is that your college days be spent in the quest for autonomy. If you are successful, you will certainly be able to recognize a wise person when you encounter one. That *is* guaranteed.

Index